M000217807

THE PIOUS UNION OF
OF
ST. JOSEPH

Pious Union In Honor Of

ST. JOSEPH

patron of a Happy Death

For
The Salvation of the Dying

By
Rev. Hugolinus Storff, O.F.M.

MEDIATRIX PRESS

MMXVIII

ISBN: 978-1-953746-65-8

Nihil obstat:
P. T. Gelinas,
    Censor.
Chicago, Jan. 11, 1930.

Imprimatur:
✠ George Cardinal Mundelein,
    Archbishop of Chicago.
Chicago, Jan. 16, 1930.

Imprimi potest:
Fr. Vincent Schrempp, O.F.M.
    Min. Prov.

© Mediatrix Press, 2018
The Pious Union of St. Joseph was first published in 1919 and is in the public domain. Typesetting for the current edition is copyrighted by Mediatrix Press and may not be reproduced in electronic or physical format for commercial purposes. Photocopies are allowed for any educational or religious use.

Cover art:
Joseph mit Christusknaben
Öl auf Leinwand

Table of Contents

Episcopal Approvals

Approval of the
Most Rev. Archbishop of St. Louis, Mo.

Archbishop's House,
St. Louis, Dec. 15, 1913.

My Dear Reverend Father:

I send you my good wishes for the Union, composed of the more fervent members of the society established by you some time ago for the purpose of aiding the "Dying" by their prayers. I gladly give my approval to the endorsed papers, and wish you and the society success and every blessing.

Yours sincerely,
John J. Glennon, Archbishop of St Louis.

Approval of the
Most Rev. Archbishop of San Francisco, Cal.

Office of the Archbishop
San Francisco, Christmas Eve, 1919

My Dear Father Provincial:

With my most cordial approval of your work in behalf of the poor sinners in the throes of death, goes also my fervent prayer for the success of the Pious Union which your zeal has done so much to promote. With every wish for a happy blessed Christmas Believe me, dear Father.

Yours ever devotedly in Christ,

Edward J. Hanna. Archbishop of San Francisco.

Diocese of Monterey and Los Angeles.
Los Angeles, Cal., September 10, 1919.

My Dear Father Hugolinus:

It must be a great consolation to you, as it is to all who have learned to know that your work for the salvation of the dying is enlisting the sympathy of so many people. Happily have you chosen St. Joseph as Patron of the Pious Union for the Salvation of the Dying. He, more than the other children of men, was blessed with the grace of a happy death. I hope the book which you have so carefully prepared and which has the approbation of the distinguished Archbishop of San Francisco, will do much to spread this devotion. There are in all of our communities a number of devoted souls who will willingly consecrate themselves, their prayers and good works to the salvation of dying souls. I hope to see this Union spread among the parishes of the diocese of Monterey and Los Angeles. Believe me.

Yours very devotedly,

John J. Cantwell, Bishop of Monterey and Los Angeles.

Approbation of the Most Rev. Father General of the Franciscan Order.
Rome, January 17, 1914.

The Lord give thee Peace!

After receiving the documents, relating to the "Pious Union in honor of St. Joseph, Patron of a Happy Death, for the Salvation of the Dying," which you sent me with your letter of Dec. 12th, I myself carefully read them and thereupon entrusted the same to another Father for examination.

Whereas it is evident that nothing opposed to faith or good morals is contained in said documents, but on the contrary much good, and that of the greatest importance, can be expected from this Union, I gladly impart to said work and the organization, as far as lies in my power, my approval together with the Seraphic

Blessing, in order that from day to day it may become more and more widely spread among the faithful who with their whole heart will devote themselves to the work, thus to assist the Dying in life's last decisive struggle, upon which their eternity depends and to open to them the gates of everlasting happiness.

May Christ Jesus dying for us on the Cross and St. Joseph, the Patron of the Dying, bless the work and bestow upon the well-deserving members, an abundant reward.

Imparting to you my blessing with paternal affection, I remain in the Sacred Heart of Jesus,

Your most devoted,

Fr. Pacificus,

Minister General.

Approvals given to The Little Company of
St. Joseph for the Dying

Approved:

Edward J. Hanna, Archbishop of San Francisco.
March 2, 1923

Fr. Turibius Deaver, O.F.M., Min. Prov.

March 9, 1923

Approbation of the Little Company of St.
Joseph for the Dying, specially blessed by His
Holiness, Pope Pius XI, given by the Most Rev.
Minister General of the Franciscan Order.
Curia Generalis, Rome, Italy.

Very Rev. and Dear Father:

Fully confirming the approbation given by the former
Minister General, the Most Rev. P. Pacificus Monza, to
the Pious Union of St. Joseph, I also heartily approve its
new organization, the Little Company of St. Joseph for
the Salvation of the Poor Dying Sinners, formed for the
more fervent and active members of the Pious Union of
St. Joseph.

I warmly recommend this noble and charitable work
to all the children and lovers of our Holy Father St.
Francis whose heart was ever burning with love and
zeal for the conversion and salvation of the poor
sinners, the poorest of whom are undoubtedly the dying
sinners.

Let us confidently hope that the Little Company will
be a powerful means of reanimating devotion to St.
Joseph, which was so much propagated in former days

by the great Saints of our Order.

Praying therefore St. Joseph, the most chaste Spouse of our Immaculate Mother Mary, to spread his Little Company for the Poor Dying Sinners in the entire Franciscan family, I gladly give to this Little Company and to all its members and promoters the Seraphic Blessing.

Given on the Feast of the Patronage of St. Joseph, Rome, April 17, 1929.

F. Bonaventure Marrani, O.F.M.
Minister General

To the Very Rev. P. Hugolinus Joseph Storff, O.F.M.
Def. Gen.

Note:—The members of the Little Company of St. Joseph for the Dying who are fully inscribed, thereby become also members of the Primary Pious Union of the Death of St. Joseph in Rome, as was expressly stated by the Director General of the Pious Union in Rome. Since the Little Company of St. Joseph now forms an integral part of the Primary Pious Union of St. Joseph in Rome, the members of the Little Company can gain all the Indulgences and Privileges granted by the Popes to the Primary Pious Union of St. Joseph erected in the Church of the Death of St. Joseph in Rome.

THE PIOUS UNION AND THE LITTLE COMPANY OF ST. JOSEPH FOR THE DYING

The Pious Union of St. Joseph was founded many years ago for the purpose of effectually helping the Dying to obtain through the intercession of St. Joseph, the Patron of the Dying, the grace of a Happy Death.

The Little Company of St. Joseph for the Dying consists of those fervent members of the Pious Union of St. Joseph who have formally made the Act of Consecration of their life and of their life's work for the Salvation of the Poor Dying Sinners.

The members of the Little Company really consider the Salvation of the Poor Dying Sinners the main object of their life. Under the guidance and protection of St. Joseph, the Patron of the Dying, their whole life shall be a continual pleading with the Mercy of God for the Salvation of the Poor Dying Sinners.

The Little Company of St. Joseph was organized December 12, 1920, in commemoration of the Golden Jubilee Year of St. Joseph, which by order of Pope Benedict XV began December 8. The Holy Father urgently requested all pastors of souls to promote devotion to St. Joseph as Patron of the Dying. In the beautiful Encyclical specially written for that solemn occasion for the Salvation of the Agonizing, the Holy Father says: "Since he (St. Joseph) is held in great honor as the helper of the Dying, because our Lord Himself and His Blessed Mother were present at his deathbed, the pastors of souls should do their utmost to promote and support with the prestige of their authority all the pious societies formed to obtain the help of St. Joseph for the benefit of the Dying".

Difference Between the Little Company and the Pious Union of St. Joseph

The members of the Pious Union pray in general for the dying and are requested to say every morning and evening the following prayer:

O St. Joseph, Foster-father of Jesus Christ and true Spouse of the Virgin Mary, pray for us and for the Dying of this day (night). Amen.

The members of the Little Company, besides being members of he Pious Union, make an Act of Consecration, by which they offer their life and the good works of their life for the Poor Dying Sinners to save them from hell. This Act of Consecration for the Dying is generally made before the Blessed Sacrament exposed and is always followed by an Act of

Consecration to St. Joseph, the Patron of the Dying. When these Acts can not be made publicly in the meeting of the Little Company, they may be made privately before a statue, picture or altar of St. Joseph.

The full name and address should be sent to the Director. No fee is required to become a member, since all expenses of this Society are paid by free donations of members who are willing and able to help the good cause.

Conditions for Actual Membership
Pious Union:
To pray for the dying.
To have full name registered.
Little Company of St. Joseph:
To make the act of Consecration.
To have full name registered.

Special Recommendations for the Members

1. To show a special love for this work and to consider the Salvation of the Poor Dying Sinners the great object of one's life and work.
2. To strive to lead a truly Christian life and to perform all duties with a good intention, out of

obedience and love of God.

3. Frequently to call God's Mercy on the Dying Sinners by saying for them: "My Jesus, Mercy!" (300 days Indulgence each time.)

4. At every Holy Mass you hear to offer up at the Consecration the Most Precious Blood of Jesus Christ for the Salvation of the Dying Sinners.

5. To receive Holy Communion frequently, even daily, and either to offer it up for the Dying Sinners, or at least to pray for the Dying Sinners immediately after receiving Holy Communion.

6. To remember specially the thousands of Poor Dying Children who are in danger of dying without Holy Baptism and can not save themselves.

7. To ask and encourage others to help in this good work either by joining the Little Company or by having Holy Masses said in honor of St. Joseph for the Poor Dying Sinners.

Affiliation of the Pious Union in Honor of St. Joseph for the Salvation of the Dying to the Primary Pious Union in Rome

This Pious Union already existed some years, when Pope Pius X, by an Apostolic Letter, dated February 12, 1914, raised a similar Association, erected in the newly built church of St. Joseph in Rome, to the dignity of an Arch-Confraternity with the faculty of aggregating similar Societies, so that they may also enjoy all the Indulgences and Privileges granted to the Arch-Confraternity.

In this Apostolic Letter Pope Pius X speaks of the purpose of the Society in Honor of St. Joseph for the Dying in these beautiful words: "Desirous to show more manifestly how much we consider the purpose of this Society worthy of every praise, We wish that Our name be inscribed first of all among the members of the same and at the same time We exhort all the beloved Brethren of the Priesthood not to neglect daily to remember in the Divine Sacrifice those who are hard pressed by the struggle of death, and, furthermore, We advise all the faithful, especially the religious men and women, that they accustom themselves to pour forth special prayers to God and to St. Joseph for the Dying;

for, if it is a holy and wholesome thought to pray for the dead who, though delivered to the cleansing flames, have reached the port of Salvation, it seems to be no less commendable solicitude to implore help from heaven for those miserable ones that are placed in the last conflict upon which depends their eternity."

What better commendation could be given to this work? But, in order to obtain for the members of this Pious Union some special Indulgences and Privileges, the Pious Union was canonically erected in the Franciscan Church of St. Anthony of Padua, St. Louis, Mo., with permission of the Most Rev. Archbishop J. J. Glennon.

Thereupon, application for affiliation was made to the Director of the Pious Union in Rome, which, by a Brief of Pope Pius X, dated February 12, 1914, had been raised to a Primary Society with the faculty of aggregating similar associations. The request being granted, the Pious Union erected in St. Anthony's Church was duly affiliated to the Arch-Confraternity of the Church of the Death of St. Joseph in Rome on July 19, 1914.

With the kind permission of the Most Rev. Archbishop of San Francisco, Cal., E. J. Hanna, the Pious Union was also canonically erected and duly affiliated to the Primary Union at Rome, in the Franciscan church of St. Boniface, San Francisco, Cal., 133 Golden Gate Avenue.

The permission of His Eminence George Cardinal Mundelein, Archbishop of Chicago, has been granted for the canonical erection of the Pious Union for the Dying in St. Peter's church, corner Clark and Polk Sts., Chicago, Ill.

As is stated in the Diploma of Affiliation, the members of our Pious Union who are duly enrolled, are made sharers in all the Indulgences, Privileges, and Spiritual Blessings granted to the Arch-Confraternity in Rome.

The following Indulgences may be gained under the usual conditions:

1) Plenary Indulgence on the day of enrollment.

2) Plenary Indulgence on the two feasts of St. Joseph, the 19th of March and the feast of his-Patronage.

3) Plenary Indulgence for hearing Mass and receiving Holy Communion for a dying member.

4) Plenary Indulgence at the moment of death. (By invoking the name of Jesus.)

5) 300 days every morning and evening for reciting the ejaculatory prayer given below: O St. Joseph, etc.

6) 100 days for every act of charity and devotion performed according to the intention of the Society.

7) The members, moreover, share in all the Masses and services held in the Church dedicated to the Death of St. Joseph in Rome, in the spiritual privileges of the

Congregation of the Servants of Charity, to whom this Church is confided, and in the good works of all the religious Orders affiliated to the Pious Onion.

It is heartily recommended to the Priests to make a special Memento for the Dying in every Mass, and to the faithful to say a special prayer for the Dying at every Holy Communion and to recite the ejaculatory prayer: "O St. Joseph, etc." ... after their morning and evening prayers; moreover, to say seven "Glory be to the Father, etc."... in honor of the seven Joys and Sorrows of St. Joseph every Wednesday, and to make a novena or triduum before the feasts of the Holy Family, the Espousals, the Death, and the Patronage of St. Joseph.

Ejaculatory Prayer

 St. Joseph Foster-father of Jesus Christ and true spouse of the Virgin Mary, pray for us and for the Dying of this day (night). Amen.

Act of Consecration for the Dying

I promise to Almighty God, the dear Lord in the Blessed Sacrament, our Immaculate Mother Mary, St. Joseph, our Patron (our holy Father St. Francis), and my

Guardian Angel, to consecrate my whole life and life's work for the Salvation of the Poor Dying Sinners, especially those who on account of mortal sin are in the greatest and proximate danger of being eternally lost. As far as I can and my other obligations permit, I now give and offer up through the hands of Mary Immaculate and St. Joseph all my good works, prayers, and sacrifices in union with the Precious Blood of Jesus Christ and all the Holy Masses, that they may continually plead for the Dying and obtain for them all the graces necessary and conducive to their eternal Salvation. In union with the Loving and Agonizing Heart of Jesus I wish to live, work, and die for them. My Jesus, Mercy! Amen.

(To be made privately or publicly before an altar or statue of St. Joseph.)

Act of Consecration to
St. Joseph Patron of the Dying

LESSED Joseph, faithful Guardian of my Redeemer, Jesus Christ, protector of thy chaste spouse, the Virgin Mother of God, and best Patron of the Dying, I choose thee this day to be my special Patron and Helper for the work of saving the Poor Dying Sinners. I firmly resolve to honor thee all the days of my life and to pray and work for the Salvation of the Dying under thy guidance and powerful protection.

Therefore I humbly beseech thee to receive me as thy client, to instruct me in every affliction, to obtain for me and others the knowledge and love of the Heart of Jesus and Mary, and finally to defend and protect me and all poor sinners at the hour of death.

Amen.

FIRST PART
THE SALVATION OF THE DYING AND
A HAPPY HOUR OF DEATH

I. Object of the Work

DEAR FRIEND AND KIND READER:

Did you ever seriously consider that the most important grace for every man is the grace of a happy death, that means, a death in the love and friendship of a merciful God? Although all would like to die well, yet how few even think of duly preparing or properly working for it! To many death comes as an utter surprise, since it finds them entirely unprepared. And yet, upon the moment of death will depend an eternity of either unspeakable happiness in heaven or greatest misery in hell. Should Christian prudence not move you to provide in due time the best possible means of securing for yourself the grace of a happy death? However, we must not forget that this grace of final perseverance can not be merited in the strict sense of the word, as it is a special gift of God's mercy and kindness. But this great mercy of God will not be refused to those whom God himself promised it. For Jesus Christ Himself has said: "Blessed are the merciful, for they shall obtain mercy and: "With what measure you mete, it shall be measured to you again." Firmly relying on these promises of Christ, every Christian who sincerely wishes to obtain a happy death, should strive most earnestly to render God merciful to his soul by performing works of mercy for his neighbor. Which, then, is the best and greatest work of mercy that we can perform for our neighbor at any time, no matter in what circumstances we may be? It is the work especially recommended in this little book: "The Salvation of the Poor Dying Sinners." The purpose of this little book is, therefore, to help the Poor Dying Sinners and, by daily imploring the mercy of God, to save as many of them as possible. By this work of mercy, faithfully practised till the end of our life, we confidently hope to obtain the same mercy of God at the moment of our own death. As St. Joseph is the special Patron of the Dying, he shall be our Model, Leader, and Protector in this work.

Dear friend and kind reader, take this little book; read, pray, reflect seriously, and then resolve courageously to help this work of mercy as much as you can, for the honor and love of God, for your own welfare, and for the eternal Salvation of many immortal souls. May Jesus, the merciful Savior of all poor sinners, move your charitable heart and say to you, as he said in the Gospel: "This do, and thou shalt live."

II. The Number of the Dying

Do you know how many persons die every day, every week, every month, and every year in the whole world? According to the most reliable statistics, every day about 140,000 die and must appear before the judgment-seat of God. This means that every second at least one person is dying; every minute about 100 persons, every hour nearly 6,000, every day about 140,000, every week about one million, every month about 4 millions, and every year about 50 millions of men die, which is about the 35th part of the whole human race. What a great number! And some day in the future you will be one of them. Who knows how soon? Every moment then some person is dying and is perhaps in the greatest danger of being lost forever. Does this not clearly show you that this work of charity and mercy is continually needed, more than any other? What we need now, is a number of fervent Christians who will daily, nay hourly, pray for the Dying Sinners, even if it is but the short ejaculation: "My Jesus, mercy on the Poor Dying Sinners!" What is still better, is a number of truly charitable and heroic souls, who will not only pray, but also continually work for the Dying and by the Act of Consecration make of their whole life a constant pleading to the throne of Mercy for the Salvation of the

Dying. Thou will surely one day belong to the number of the Dying. Will you not also belong to the number of those who try hard to save the Poor Dying Sinners. Now ask your charitable heart: "How many would you like to save?" The more you will save, the surer will be your own salvation, for those who have been saved by your prayers and good works will pray and plead also for you at the moment of your own death. Therefore come, join the pious Union, and even induce others to take up this good work; the more members we get, the better it will be. Although our number is yet small compared with the great number of the Dying, still we can do a great deal for their salvation, because God Himself will help us as long as we wish and try to do His work.

"Pray for one another that you may be saved. He that causes a sinner to be converted shall save his soul from death and shall cover a multitude of sin."

III. The Religious Condition of the Dying

How many of the dying, do you think, are in the state of sanctifying grace and actually prepared for a good death? There are about 1,600 millions of human beings living on the earth. Of these about one-half, that is 800,000,000, are still pagan, not knowing or at least not honoring the one true God; millions do not believe in Jesus Christ and His great work of redemption, as the Jews and Muslims (over 200 millions).

Of the Christians, we find about 300 millions separated from the only true Church of Christ; namely, all the different Protestant and Schismatical sects. Thus of the 1,600 millions of men only about 250 millions belong to the Catholic Church and profess the true faith of Jesus Christ. If we now carefully consider the spiritual and religious condition of the Catholics, we find that a great many are Catholics only in name, because they do not practice their holy religion. How few properly prepare for death by leading a truly Catholic life and by conscientiously fulfilling all their religious duties! This sad religious condition of the world can in no way be attributed to God, but must be ascribed to the sins and crimes of the different nations and of men. The grace of the true faith was offered to all nations. It was also offered in some way to all men. But what has happened?

These nations or men either rejected the light and grace of faith, or afterwards lost it through their fault or the fault of their ancestors. Although we do not want to judge or condemn anyone in particular, yet we can not help thinking that perhaps most or at least very many of the dying are not in the state of sanctifying grace, or are not well prepared for the last moment, and thus in the greatest danger of being eternally lost. And all could be saved. All that is needed is the worthy reception of the Holy Sacraments or a good act of perfect contrition. This may in many cases require a special, even an extraordinary grace of God, which your charity, your prayers, your good works, your sacrifices will obtain for them. In such a way you may perhaps save many immortal souls for all eternity. What a vast field of action for your charitable heart! Should this consideration not animate you to increased fervor to promote this work of charity and mercy? Everywhere interest in the Missions both at home and in foreign countries is awakening or increasing. Help this movement by your charity according to your means. But know that you can best help the missionaries and even become a missionary yourself by trying to save every day the thousands of Poor Dying Sinners. It is principally the grace of God that effects the conversion of sinners, and this grace is best obtained by prayer, good works, and sacrifices.

You may thus save as many and perhaps even more than a missionary by his exterior work. Will you now join the ranks of true apostolic laborers and help the good cause with all zeal and fervor? Do not hesitate any longer, for every moment is precious. As the Act of

Consecration is the best way of helping the dying continually, a short explanation of this Act will now be given.

IV. About the Act of Consecration for the Dying

It is urged by the rules of the Union that the members try to be always in the state of sanctifying grace and to perform all their actions in the spirit of obedience and true love of God and for the same intention that Christ, the Savior, had in all His actions and sufferings, namely the honor of God, His Father, and the eternal salvation of man. Christ, however, honored His Father most and became our Savior principally by shedding His blood and by dying for us, poor sinners.

As good Christians we should try to return this love to Christ by showing the same love to our neighbor; we should try to become, like Christ, another savior for our neighbor. This is done in a general way by praying and working for the conversion of sinners. But no one will deny that, of all the poor sinners, the Dying Sinners are most in need of our help. Severe sickness, entire exhaustion, corporal and mental suffering, the dread of Impending judgment, the uncertainty of the future lot, terrible temptations of the devil, who uses once more his utmost endeavors to ruin the soul for ever, may make the agony, or death struggle, very hard, perhaps more so in the soul than in the body. The Catholic Church, as a good mother tries to help her dying children by the last Sacraments and the assistance of the priest at the last moment. But what about the thousands every day who can not receive the Holy Sacraments and will not have the assistance of a priest when they are dying? The hour of decision is at hand and death is the most important moment of our whole life, because a never-ending eternity will depend upon it. You can, therefore, show no greater love or mercy to your neighbor than by trying to procure for him the grace of a happy death. At the same time you will show the greatest love for your dying Savior.

If on the day of the last judgment Christ will say to those who fed their hungry neighbor: "I was hungry, and you gave me to eat," He will in like manner say to those who help and assist their dying neighbor: "I was dying and you helped and assisted me. Amen, I say to you, as long as you did it to one of these my least brethren, you did it to Me." The Dying Sinners should therefore represent to you Christ dying laden with all our sins and you should piously believe that whatever you do to help the dying, Christ will consider it as being done to Him, agonizing in the Garden of Olives and dying on the Cross.

All these considerations will clearly show why for the members of the Union the special intention of all their good works and prayers should be: "To save the Dying Sinners." But to help the dying continually, all our good works, even our whole life, should be devoted to this great cause. This, we think, is best done by the Act of Consecration and Offering for the Dying. What, then, do we really offer to God by this Act? We must know that every good work, performed in the state of sanctifying grace and with a good intention, will produce a threefold good fruit:

1) The fruit of real merit; this means, we merit an increase in sanctifying grace and of our glory in heaven. This fruit of our good works remains always a personal merit and can never be given to any other person.

2) The fruit of satisfaction, by which we atone for our past offences and satisfy Divine Justice for the punishments deserved for our sins. This fruit of our good works may be given to the Poor Souls in Purgatory, who must still atone and suffer for their past offences. The so-called "Heroic Act for the Poor Souls" consists in this that a person gives to God through the hands of Mary all the satisfactions of the good works performed by him that God may apply these satisfactions to the Poor Souls to shorten their time of

suffering and deliver them from purgatory.

3) The fruit of impetration, by which we obtain new actual graces that may help us to avoid sin, to overcome difficulties and temptations, to perform other good works, and to persevere in doing good till the end. The third fruit of our good works by which actual graces are obtained, may also be offered for other living persons; for it is Catholic doctrine that by prayers and good works we may obtain actual graces not only for ourselves, but also for others. The Act of Consecration for the Dying consists in this, that, as far as we are not bound to pray and work for ourselves or others, the fruit of impetration of all our prayers and good works shall be offered to God for the Salvation of the Poor Dying Sinners. To meet some objections that might be made against this Act, the following points should be well considered:

1) This Act for the Dying is entirely compatible with the Heroic Act for the Poor Souls. For by the Heroic Act for the Poor Souls we can give them only the satisfactory merit of our good works. However, by the Act for the Dying we wish to obtain actual graces for the eternal Salvation of the Dying.

But the Poor Souls are safe for all eternity, and can not receive any more graces, since with the moment of death the time of grace has elapsed. Both Acts may therefore be made at the same time, if a person wishes to do so, to help both the living and the dead.

2) The Act for the Dying does not hinder any one of us from praying for some other intention or some other person for whom we are bound or wish to pray. For this reason the words: "As far as I am able and my other obligations permit" were expressly inserted in the Act. But consider that so many prayers, devotions, and good works are performed without any special intention or application and by making the Act all these prayers and good works will be offered for the Dying. Besides, we may have several good intentions in our prayers and good works and thus we can always include the dying in the good works and prayers that are offered for others.

3) If it is said that we continually need the grace of God to work out our own salvation, we answer that this is true indeed; but mind well that Jesus Christ expressly said: "Thou shalt love thy neighbor as thyself." Therefore true charity will work as hard for the salvation of one's neighbor as for one's own salvation. Know also that God is infinite in bounty, and, in response to our prayers and works of charity, He will

gladly give His graces not only to us, but also to the dying, if with true Christian charity we always include them and thus desire not only our own salvation, but also the salvation of our neighbor.

4) Never forget that our eternal salvation will principally depend upon the mercy of God. But the surest way of securing the mercy of God for us is to show mercy to our neighbor, as Christ Himself has said: "Blessed are the merciful, for they shall obtain mercy." Again: "Take heed, what you hear: With what measure you shall mete, it shall be measured to you again." Now there is no greater act of true mercy and charity for our neighbor than continual endeavor to work for his eternal salvation.

Of all our suffering brethren the dying are perhaps the most neglected, although they are in the greatest need of our help. How many Masses are daily said for the Poor Souls in Purgatory, but how few for the Salvation of the Dying! Yet the Poor Souls are safe for all eternity, but every day many of the Dying Sinners are in the greatest and immediate danger of being eternally lost. Your charity may save at least some of them. Which is, then, greater work of charity: "To free a Poor Soul from Purgatory, or to save a Dying Sinner from eternal hell-fire?"

6) The Act of Consecration for the Dying shall even make the Salvation of the Dying the main object of our whole life and of our life's work. As an artist lives for his art, continually works for it and tries to make the best success of it, thus we wish to live, to work, and even to die for the Salvation of the Dying. Our life should be a continual sacrifice for them. Even our death accepted with perfect resignation to God's holy will in union with the death of Christ shall be offered to God to help those who will be dying at the same time.

7) To render this Act the more efficacious, we should unite our prayers, good work, and the sacrifices, first, with the Precious Blood of Christ, as it is the price of our redemption, and, secondly, with all the holy Masses that are celebrated every day, since in Holy Mass Christ continually renews the Sacrifice of the Cross and offers again His Body and Blood for the remission of sins. We are, then, praying and working in union with our blessed Savior who promised us: "Whatever you shall ask the Father in my name, that He will give you." Knowing moreover our sinfulness and unworthiness, we make the offering of the Act through the hands of Mary Immaculate and St. Joseph. In her Immaculate Conception Mary conquered the devil and crushed his head. The Immaculate Conception shall also obtain the

victory over the devil in the souls of the dying, and Mary will thus prove to be the best Mother of the Poor Dying Sinners. Since St. Joseph is the Patron of the Dying, he was chosen to be the special Protector of this work, who, with Mary, will present our Act of Offering to God.

8) Therefore, the real meaning of the Act of Consecration for the Dying is this: "Without making a vow, we promise, as far as we can, and our other obligations permit, to give to God through the hands of Mary Immaculate and St. Joseph all the good works, prayers, and sacrifices of our whole life for the eternal Salvation of the Poor Dying Sinners." How many will you now try to save with God's grace? How many of the 140,000 persons that die every day need your helping hand to rescue them from eternal perdition?

9) Do you truly love the great St. Joseph? Then venerate him as the special Patron of the Dying, as the best Patron of a Happy Death. Since the Union was instituted in honor of St. Joseph, let the lovers of St. Joseph and the workers for the Dying attentively read the following explanation and take it to heart. May the dear St. Joseph bless this work, adopt it as his own, and crown it with success!

V. St. Joseph, the Patron of the Dying

To increase proper devotion to St. Joseph for the purpose of obtaining a happy hour of death both for ourselves and for the Poor Dying Sinners, it will be very good for the members of the Union to know why St. Joseph is considered the best Patron of the Dying.

A brief explanation of the reasons which moved the Church to give St. Joseph in the approved Litany the title "Patron of the Dying," will also show the members of this Union why St. Joseph was chosen as its principal Patron.

1) St. Joseph was the person to whom the ever-blessed Trinity entrusted its greatest treasures on earth, namely Jesus and Mary. But on Jesus and Mary rests our principal hope of eternal salvation. This ought to show us that God Himself looked upon St. Joseph as the most faithful Guardian and Protector of both the Savior and His dearest Mother Mary, and their joint work, the salvation of man. Then we, too, should entrust to St. Joseph the greatest treasure we have, our immortal soul, and its most important affair, its eternal salvation. But the salvation of our soul will chiefly depend upon our death, for a happy death in the state of sanctifying grace

will bring us eternal happiness, but an unhappy death in the state of mortal sin will cause eternal damnation. We should, therefore, entrust principally to St. Joseph the last hour of our life and the moment of our death by making him our Patron of a Happy Death.

2) St. Joseph was prefigured by Joseph of Egypt. What the Egyptian Joseph was and did for his family and the people of Egypt, St. Joseph shall be and do for his family and his people in the New Law. As Joseph of Egypt was called in the language of the Egyptians, "the Savior of the world," thus St. Joseph shall become for us a Savior by obtaining the grace of a happy death. As Joseph of Egypt was made the first minister of king Pharaoh, thus St. Joseph is now the first minister of our heavenly king, Jesus Christ. This Heavenly King directs us in our greatest need to St. Joseph, and like the king of Egypt says to us: "Go to Joseph and do all that he shall say to you." Whenever we resemble the people of Egypt and are in danger of dying an eternal death on account of spiritual want and famine, St. Joseph should give us the heavenly bread, Jesus Christ, to preserve our soul to life everlasting. In their great need the people of Egypt said to Joseph "Give us bread, why should we die in thy presence? ... Our life is in thy hand, only let my lord look favorably upon us, and we will gladly serve the

king." In like manner we should pray to St. Joseph: "O, St. Joseph, our life is in thy hand, thou are our Patron, protect us by thy presence from eternal death, look now favorably upon us, give us Christ, our best bread, and we will gladly serve Him, our heavenly king."

3) But the dignity and power of St. Joseph is by far greater than that of Joseph of Egypt. St. Joseph is the Foster-father of Jesus Christ, the Son of God. Thus St. Joseph alone shares in the dignity of the heavenly Father. Both Jesus and Mary call him by that sweet name, "Father." Mary said to Jesus when she found Him in the temple: "Son, why hast Thou done so to us? Behold, thy father and I have sought thee sorrowing." Besides St. Joseph is also the spouse of the Blessed Virgin Mary and the head of the Holy Family of God on earth. With this threefold high dignity and power given to no other saint of God, St. Joseph must indeed be the best Patron of the Dying, the best Patron of a happy death. For we can only be saved, if we die as the adopted children of God, our heavenly Father, as the spiritual children of Mary, our heavenly Mother, and as living members of the great family of God on earth, the Holy Catholic Church. But it is clear that no one is better fitted to obtain these graces and favors for us at the hour of our death than St. Joseph.

If at the moment of death, St. Joseph is our spiritual foster-father, and we his foster-children, he will see that we also die as the children of God, the heavenly Father, whose place he took on earth and with whom he alone shares the sweet name "Father of Jesus." Besides, St. Joseph, being the spouse of Mary, is best fitted to make us the spiritual children of Mary. No other saint is so closely united with Mary as St. Joseph. The two are like one heart and one soul. Mary will then be the special loving Mother of those who at death are the spiritual children of St. Joseph. Whom St. Joseph loves, also Mary will love. Moreover, St. Joseph is also the special Patron of the Universal Church, the present family of God on earth.

The patron of the Church will take the best care that his devoted children and clients will die as good members of the Catholic Church, the family of God, now specially entrusted to him. Know then that if you wish to die as a good Christian, you must like Christ be under the special care and protection of St. Joseph, if you wish to die as a true child of Mary, you must be a foster-child of St. Joseph, and if you wish to die as a good Catholic, St. Joseph, the Patron of the Catholic Church, must be your special Patron at your death. Thus it is clear that St. Joseph is best fitted to be the Patron of the Dying.

4) St. Joseph will gladly do for his spiritual children what he did for the Child Jesus, which again points him out as the best Patron of the Dying. When the wicked king Herod sought to kill the Infant Jesus, St. Joseph saved the Savior for us by fleeing to Egypt. But this work of saving the life of Christ from the danger of death was entrusted by God to St. Joseph.

Thus, when we are in danger of losing the Savior and our eternal life, especially at the hour of death, on account of the most wicked and cruel king, the devil, so well figured by Herod, we shall be safe, if we are under the special protection of St. Joseph, since he will guard the life of the Savior in our soul by frustrating the evil designs of the devil. It was also St. Joseph, who with great sorrow sought Jesus after the child was lost, and found Him again after three days in the temple. In like manner, if we should have the misfortune of losing Jesus by mortal sin, let us call upon St. Joseph that he, as our Patron, may help us to seek Jesus as our Patron, may help us to seek Jesus in the sorrow of our heart by an act of perfect Contrition and a sincere Confession and find Him again in the temple of our own heart by a worthy, holy Communion. If St. Joseph is our Patron of a Happy Death, he will surely help us not to lose Jesus at the moment of death, but to find Him then as a loving, merciful Savior to the greatest joy of our heart.

5) St. Joseph himself had the most happy death, for, as tradition relates, he died in the arms of Jesus and of Mary. He therefore best knows what it means to die a holy and a happy death; he also knows that this is the greatest grace and favor God can bestow on any man. Therefore, if he is our Patron, he will try to obtain this grace and favor for his devoted children. As to the power of St. Joseph, there can be no doubt that it is very great in heaven, for Jesus who had been obedient to St. Joseph on earth, will even obey him in heaven, at least not refuse him any petition in favor of his children. We must not forget that next to the Blessed Virgin Mary no one stood in closer relation to Jesus on earth than St. Joseph. We may then safely say that a good child and client of St. Joseph will not be lost. For this reason we should choose him as our special Patron of a Happy Death and invoke him every day as the great Patron of the Dying.

6) But nothing will please St. Joseph more than if we try to imitate his holy example, by becoming also Patrons of the Dying, in consecrating our whole life for the Salvation of the Dying. This is the reason why we have chosen St. Joseph as the special Patron for our

Union, and we do not doubt that the dear St. Joseph will prove to be our powerful helper and protector in this great work of saving the Poor Dying Sinners. But what will be our reward as members of this Union? If we work hard with the kind and powerful assistance of St. Joseph daily to save as many as we can, St. Joseph will recognize us as his best children, both at the moment of death and before the judgment-seat of God. Jesus, called "the Son of St. Joseph," will not condemn those whom St. Joseph will present to Him as his special devoted children and clients. You ask for your reward? If you faithfully imitate St. Joseph as Patron of the Dying, you may confidently hope that he will bring Jesus and Mary to your deathbed, that you may die like him in their sweet embrace. What a strong incentive to join this Union and be a faithful member, that means, to be a most zealous worker for the Salvation of the Poor Dying Sinners under the Patronage of St. Joseph!

Remember well that every day over 100,000 persons die and perhaps most of them are in the greatest danger of being eternally lost; therefore, in the greatest need of our help. St. Joseph will gladly help us in a work so dear to him and he will also see to our proper reward. Those who join this Union should have their name inscribed in the Register and then make the Act of Consecration before an altar or statue of St. Joseph and renew it from time to time, especially, on the feasts of St. Joseph. Special prayers are given in this book for the convenience of the lovers of St. Joseph, to help them in their devotion to this great Saint and powerful Protector. Let the members of this Union often say with great confidence and fervor: "St. Joseph, Patron of a happy death, pray for us and the Poor Dying Sinners. Amen."

VI. An Appeal to Catholic Children

Dear Catholic Children, consider well what special favors and graces the good God has bestowed upon you, that you were born of good Catholic parents, received the holy Sacrament of Baptism, and were permitted even at an early age to receive the dear Jesus into your young and innocent hearts. Did you ever sincerely thank the good God for these special favors? To show your gratitude, begin now to pray every day for all the Poor Dying Sinners, especially for the thousands of Poor Dying Children. Many of these children are in the greatest danger of dying in original sin, without the grace of Holy Baptism, which would exclude them forever from the joys of Heaven. Again, many of the Dying Children that have been baptized and have arrived at the use of their reason, may have already committed mortal sin, and not being Catholics, not being well instructed, and not being properly prepared for death, are in the greatest danger of being eternally lost. What a beautiful chance to become even in your young days Missionaries, that means, helpers of the dear Jesus and of the priests in the great work of saving souls for heaven. You shall principally save the Dying Children. Pray, then, every day for the thousands of little Dying Children that they may not die without Holy Baptism. Pray also for the grown-up Dying Children that they may either receive the Holy Sacraments or make an Act of Perfect Contrition before they die. Oh! How many could you thus save for all eternity, as the number of Dying Children is very great every day. Dear Catholic Child! If you never committed a mortal sin, know that you baptismal innocence is a great power with God, your best Father in Heaven, and your fervent prayers coming from a pure, innocent heart will help very much the good cause of saving the Poor Dying Sinners.

Resolve, therefore, with the help of the good Jesus to preserve the innocence of your soul and never consent to the bad, shameful sin of impurity. Show yourself also grateful to your parents. Ask the good Jesus to preserve and bless your kind parents and, when He will call them from this life, to give them the grace of a happy death.

They took the best care of your temporal and bodily life. How nice would it be, if your prayers would bring them eternal life and happiness! If your father or any member of your family should not practice his religion, or not belong to the Catholic faith, pray every day for his conversion. To obtain this great favor, pray daily for the Poor Dying Sinners and tell the dear Jesus to reward you by granting all the members of your family the grace of the true faith and the grace of a happy death. You will be then the Missionary of your family. Never stop praying, never get discouraged, perhaps your prayer will yet be heard at the last hour. Unlimited confidence in the Infinite Mercy of our best Father in Heaven and of the good Shepherd, Jesus Christ, will work miracles of conversion, especially if good, innocent children will pray and offer their pure lives for this great cause. Love the dear St. Joseph, ask him to be the head of your family, tell him to bless your father's work and business, to help your good mother at home, and to make you a good, pious, and obedient child, that you may always resemble the child Jesus Who was so good and obedient to St. Joseph and Mary.

Dear Catholic Mothers! Read this to your children, explain it to them, make them live this devotion, and say the prayers for the Dying with them. Jesus will then specially bless you in your children.

VII. An Urgent Request to Priests and Pastors of Souls

Every priest and pastor will more or less be called upon to attend Sick calls and *Dying Persons*. There is no greater consolation for a fervent priest and pastor than the thought that the Sick and the *Dying* of his congregation all died well prepared. But in every congregation eases may occur that cause great anxiety and grief to the heart of the priest: Sudden deaths, unconscious dying persons, hardened sinners who refuse to admit the priest or to receive the Sacraments, Catholics to whom for grave reasons the Sacraments cannot be administered. In order to obtain special graces for these Poor Dying Sinners, let the priest and pastor foster a special devotion to St. Joseph, as Patron of a Happy Death for the Salvation of the Dying Sinners, and spread this devotion among the members of his congregation, that through the special intercession of St. Joseph not a single member of his congregation may die an unhappy death, but well prepared by the holy Sacraments. If there should be but one lost sheep in the congregation, let the priest follow the example of the good Shepherd who left the ninety-nine good sheep in the desert to seek the one lost sheep, and, when he finds it and succeeds in bringing it back to the fold, even at the last hour, there will be greater joy in heaven than over the ninety-nine good sheep that need no penance. A true Catholic priest will think not only of his own sheep, the Catholics of his congregation, but even of all those that do not belong to the fold. Jesus, the good Shepherd, said: "Them also must I bring." As a member of this Union, his love will be truly Catholic, that is, Universal, extending to all. If he cannot help the dying Protestants or Infidels by the exterior ministrations of his priesthood, he may yet save many of them by his fervent prayers and offerings made during Holy Mass at the Consecration and holy Communion, his visits before the tabernacle, his devout recitation of the Divine Office, and his holy priestly life. May he be able to say to God with Christ, the best model of priests: "Of them whom Thou hast given me, I have not lost any one." What joy and consolation for the good priest at the moment of death, when he is called to render an account not only of his own life, but of all those that were entrusted to his care! Make it, then, a daily practice at the elevation of the chalice in Mass to offer up through Mary Immaculate and St. Joseph the Precious Blood of Christ for the Dying.

On October 26, 1907 Pope Pius X granted an Indulgence of 100 days to Priests making a Memento in Mass for the Dying Sinners of that day.

VIII. Devotions and Prayers to St. Joseph for the Dying

The Seven Sorrows and Seven Joys of St. Joseph

This devotion owes its origin to a celebrated event, never omitted by any historian of the Saint. It is as follows: Two Franciscan Fathers were sailing along the coast of Flanders, when a terrible tempest arose, which sank the vessel with its three hundred passengers. The two Fathers had sufficient presence of mind to seize hold of a plank, upon which they were tossed to and fro upon the waves for three days and nights. In their danger and affliction their whole recourse was to St. Joseph, whom they begged for assistance in their sad condition. The Saint, thus invoked, appeared in the form of a young man of beautiful features, encouraged them to confide in his assistance and as their pilot, conducted them into a safe harbor. They, desirous to know who their benefactor was, asked his name, that they might gratefully acknowledge so great a favor and blessing. He told them he was St. Joseph, and advised them daily to recite seven times "Our Father" and "Hail Mary" in memory of his seven dolors or griefs, and of his seven joys; he then disappeared. This beautiful devotion has been specially applied for the needs of the Dying that St. Joseph, their special Patron, may safely conduct them into the harbor of eternal bliss.

The Seven Dolors and Joys of St. Joseph for the Dying

1) O glorious St. Joseph, chaste husband of most holy Mary, great was thy grief, when in a state of great uncertainty thou wast minded to put away Mary, thy stainless spouse. But how great was thy joy, when the angel revealed to thee the sublime mystery of Christ's Incarnation and the great dignity of Mary, as Mother of God. By this thy grief and thy joy we pray thee to relieve the dying of all anxieties and dreadful doubts about their future state and fill their hearts with the greatest confidence in the powerful protection of Mary, the Immaculate Mother of God. Amen.

Our Father. Hail Mary. Glory Be

V.—St. Joseph, Patron of a Happy Death,

R.—Pray for us and the Poor Dying Sinners. Amen.

2) O glorious St. Joseph, chosen Foster-father of the Word made man, great was thy grief, when thou didst see the Infant Jesus born in such extreme poverty. But how great was thy joy when thou didst behold the brightness of that holy night in which the angels sang: "Glory to God in the highest and on earth peace to men of good will." By this thy grief and thy joy, we pray thee

to obtain by thy powerful intercession for all the dying the grace that the Infant Jesus may again be born in their hearts, and that blessed with the sweet peace of God, they may also join after their death the joyful company of the angels. Amen.

Our Father. Hail Mary. Glory Be

V.—St. Joseph, Patron of a Happy Death,

R.—Pray for us and the Poor Dying Sinners. Amen.

3) O glorious St. Joseph, Model of perfect Obedience, great was thy grief, when at the Circumcision the Infant Jesus shed His first precious blood. But how great was thy joy, when thou didst give Him the sweet name of Jesus, that should bring salvation to the sinners. By this grief and thy joy we pray thee to assist the dying in their greatest need by applying to their souls the most Precious Blood of Jesus, that being cleansed from sin, they may depart with the sweet name of Jesus on their lips and in their hearts, and thus be saved for all eternity. Amen.

Our Father. Hail Mary. Glory Be

V.—St. Joseph, Patron of a Happy Death,

R.—Pray for us and the Poor Dying Sinners. Amen.

4) O glorious St. Joseph, faithful Companion of Mary, great was thy grief, when at the presentation of the

Infant in the temple thou didst hear Simeon's prophecy of the future sufferings of Jesus and of Mary. But how great was thy joy, when Simeon foretold that Jesus would be the light for the revelation of the gentiles, the glory of his people, and the resurrection of many in Israel. By this thy grief and thy joy we pray thee to assist the dying that through the light and the power of the sorrowful Mother, the dying like Simeon may also see their salvation and praise and thank God for the grace of a happy death. Amen.

Our Father. Hail Mary. Glory Be

V.—St. Joseph, Patron of a Happy Death,

R.—Pray for us and the Poor Dying Sinners. Amen.

5) O glorious St. Joseph, Protector of the Infant Jesus, great was thy grief when obeying the voice of the angel, thou didst flee with the Infant Jesus and His Mother Mary to Egypt. But how great was thy joy when at the entrance into Egypt the idols were destroyed by falling to the ground. By this thy grief and thy joy we pray thee to help the dying to banish from their hearts all idols of sinful habits, that Jesus and Mary may come and lead their souls to the land of eternal bliss. Amen.

Our Father. Hail Mary. Glory Be

V.—St. Joseph, Patron of a Happy Death,

R.—Pray for us and the Poor Dying Sinners. Amen.

6) O glorious St. Joseph, Head and Guardian of the Holy Family, great was thy grief when at the return from Egypt thou didst hear that cruel Archelaus was reigning in Judea in place of Herod. But how great was thy joy when the angel of God directed thee to go to Nazareth, where thou didst live most peacefully with Jesus and Mary till thy happy death. By this thy grief and thy joy we pray thee to assist the dying that they may overcome all attacks of the evil spirits and die peacefully under the special protection of Jesus and Mary. Amen.

Our Father. Hail Mary. Glory Be

V.—St. Joseph, Patron of a Happy Death,

R.—Pray for us and the Poor Dying Sinners. Amen.

7) O glorious St. Joseph, Best Patron of the Dying, great was thy grief when, without thy fault, thou didst lose Jesus and seek Him for three days. But how great was thy joy when thou didst find Him again in the temple. By this thy grief and thy joy we pray thee to help the dying not to lose their Savior for all eternity, but to find Him at least at the moment of death with His grace and mercy in the temple of their own hearts. Let us all die like thee in the sweet embrace of Jesus and Mary. Amen.

Our Father. Hail Mary. Glory Be
V.—St. Joseph, Patron of a Happy Death,
R.—Pray for us and the Poor Dying Sinners. Amen.

God, Who in Thy ineffable Providence has vouchsafed to choose Blessed Joseph to be the Spouse of Thy most holy Mother; grant, we beseech Thee, that we may deserve to have him for our intercessor in heaven whom on earth we venerate as our holy protector: Who lives and reigns forever and ever. Amen.

LITANY OF ST. JOSEPH
(Approved by Pope Pius X, March 18, 1909).

Lord, have mercy on us.
Christ, have mercy on us.
Lord, have mercy on us.
Christ, hear us.
Christ, graciously hear us.
God, the Father of Heaven, *have mercy on us.*
God, the Son, Redeemer of the world.
God, the Holy Ghost.
Holy Trinity, One God.
Holy Mary.   *pray for us.*
St. Joseph.
Illustrious Son of David
Light of Patriarchs.
Spouse of the Mother of God.
Chaste Guardian of the Virgin.
Foster-father of the son of God.
Watchful Defender of Christ.
Head of the Holy Family.
Joseph most just.
Joseph most chaste.
Joseph most prudent.
Joseph most valiant.

Joseph most obedient.   *Pray for us*
Joseph most faithful.
Mirror of Patience.
Lover of Poverty.
Model of workmen.
Glory of domestic life.
Guardian of virgins.
Pillar of families.
Solace of the afflicted.
Hope of the sick.
Patron of the dying.
Terror of demons.
Protector of the Holy Church.
Lamb of God, Who takest away the sins of the world, spare us, O Lord.
Lamb of God, Who takest away the sins of the world, graciously hear us, O Lord.
Lamb of God, Who takest away the sins of the world, have mercy on us,
O Lord.
V.—He hath made him the Lord of his house.
R.—And the ruler of all his possessions.

Let us pray!
O God, who in thy unspeakable providence didst deign to choose Blessed Joseph to be the spouse of Thy most

holy Mother, grant that as we venerate him as our protector on earth, we may deserve to have him as an intercessor in heaven, who livest and reignest forever and ever. Amen.

Devotion of the Seven Sundays in Honor of St. Joseph

Pope Pius granted a Plenary Indulgence on each Sunday to those who on seven consecutive Sundays, either before the feast of St. Joseph or at some other time, to obtain a great favor, will perform the devotion of the Seven Sorrows and Joys of St. Joseph, or if this can not be done, will say seven Our Fathers, seven Hail Marys and seven Glorias, and fulfill the usual conditions for gaining a Plenary Indulgence, namely, confession, communion, and prayers for our holy Mother the Church. The Indulgence is also applicable to the souls in purgatory.

Pious Salutation of St. Joseph for the Members of the Pious Union

ail, St. Joseph, full of grace, in the pious possession of Mary, thy most beloved spouse, the Lord is with thee, in Whose presence thou didst always walk and Whom thou didst serve most faithfully; blessed art thou amongst men, after Jesus their greatest honor and glory, and blessed is the fruit of thy purest spouse, Jesus, Whom thou didst so lovingly nourish, protect and carry in thy arms. Holy Joseph, chosen Foster-father of the Son of God, chaste spouse of the Immaculate Virgin Mother Mary, our best Father, and most powerful Patron of the Dying, pray for us, pray for thy chosen family, pray especially for the Poor Dying Sinners and help and protect us in all our needs of body and soul, now and at the hour of our death. Amen.

Prayer to St. Joseph for the Virtue of Purity and Chastity

GLORIOUS St. Joseph, father and protector of virgins, faithful guardian, to whose faithful care God. entrusted Jesus, Innocence itself, and Mary, the Virgin of Virgins, I pray and beseech thee, through Jesus and Mary, this double pledge which was so dear to thee, make me preserve my heart free from every stain, pure, and innocent, and make me serve Jesus and Mary forever in perfect chastity. Amen.
(100 days Indulgence, Pius IX, Feb., 3, 1863).

THE PIOUS UNION OF ST. JOSEPH

The "Memorare" in Honor of
St. Joseph.

REMEMBER, O most pure spouse of the Blessed Virgin Mary, my sweet Protector, St. Joseph: that no one ever had recourse to thy protection, or implored thy aid without obtaining relief. Confiding, therefore, in thy goodness, I come before thee and humbly supplicate thee. Despise not my petitions, Foster-father of my Redeemer, but graciously receive them. Amen.

(Indulgence of 300 days, once a day. Pius IX, June 26, 1863.)

Prayer to St. Joseph for a Happy Death

BLESSED Joseph, who didst yield thy last breath in the arms of Jesus and of Mary, when God will send death to end our career of life, come Holy Father with Jesus and Mary to aid us, and obtain this grace for us, to accept death with perfect resignation to God's holy will, and in union with the bitter death of Jesus, that by our death we may atone for our own sins and help the other Poor Dying Sinners. Let us all die in the sweet embrace of Jesus and of Mary. Into your sacred hands, Jesus, Mary, Joseph, we live and dying commend our souls. Amen.

Prayer to St. Joseph for the Dying Sinners

St. Joseph, Patron of the Dying, by the love of Jesus and of Mary, we ask thee, our best Helper and Protector, to come to the aid of all Poor Dying Sinners. Bring them the light of the true faith from God, the heavenly Father, whose place thou didst take on earth. Let them put all their hope in the blood, passion, and death of thy dear Son, Jesus Christ, our Savior. Fill their soul with the perfect love of God, the best gift of the Holy Ghost. Make them now the spiritual children of thy most chaste spouse, our dear Mother Mary Immaculate. Exercise thy power against the devil who tries his best to ruin the Dying Sinners forever. Thus we pray that by thy help and powerful intercession with Jesus and Mary, the dying may obtain the grace of a happy death. Amen.

Prayers in Honor of St. Joseph for the Agonizing.

ternal Father, by Thy love for St. Joseph, whom Thou didst select from among all men to represent Thee upon earth, have mercy on us and on the dying. Our Father, Hail Mary, Glory be to the Father.

Eternal Divine Son, by Thy love for St. Joseph, who was

Thy faithful Guardian upon earth, have mercy on us and the dying.
Our Father, Hail Mary, Glory be to the Father.

Eternal Divine Spirit, by Thy love for St. Joseph who so carefully watched over Mary, Thy beloved spouse, have mercy on us and on the dying.
Our Father, Hail Mary, Glory be to the Father.
(Indulgence of 300 days, once a day, Leo XIII, May 17, 1884).

Prayer to St. Joseph, Patron of the Dying, for Perseverance

Dear St. Joseph, Foster-father of our Divine Redeemer, and Spouse of our holy Mother, Mary Immaculate, thou didst live with them and toil for them through all the years of the hidden life, thou didst die in their arms. By the love thou bearest to them and the love they bear to thee, pray for us always and guard us. Obtain for us, O Patron of a happy death, the grace to live and die in God's love and favor, that we may spend our eternity with Jesus and Mary and with thee, O dear St. Joseph. Amen.

Novena in Honor of St. Joseph, Spouse of Mary, Most Holy

The Sovereign Pontiff, Pius IX, Nov. 28, 1876, granted to all the faithful who with contrite heart devoutly make at any time during the year a Novena in honor of St. Joseph, Spouse of Mary, most holy, with any formula of prayer, provided it be approved by competent ecclesiastical authority, an indulgence of 300 days, once a day.

Indulgenced Prayers to St. Joseph

St. Joseph, reputed father of our Lord, Jesus Christ, and true spouse of Mary, ever Virgin, pray for us.
(300 days, once a day, Leo XIII, May 15, 1891).

St. Joseph, model and patron of those who love the Sacred Heart of Jesus, pray for us.
(100 days, once a day. Leo XIII, Dec. 19, 1891).

Help us, Joseph, in our earthly strife,
E'er to lead a pure and blameless life.
(300 days, once a day. Leo XIII, March 18, 1882).

St. Joseph, friend of the Snored Heart, pray for us.
(100 days, once a day. Pius XI.)

Jesus, Mary, Joseph, I give you my heart and my soul.

Jesus, Mary, Joseph, assist me in my last agony.

Jesus, Mary, Joseph, may I breathe forth my soul in peace with you.

(300 days for all three, each time they are said. Plus VII, Aug. 26, 1814.)

Prayer to St. Joseph for the Month of October

o thee, O Blessed Joseph, we have recourse in our affliction, and after imploring the help of thy most holy Spouse, we confidently invoke thy patronage also. By that affection which united thee with the Immaculate Virgin Mother of God, and by the fatherly love with which thou didst embrace the Infant Jesus, look down, we beseech thee, with gracious eyes on the precious inheritance, which Jesus Christ purchased by His blood, and help us in our necessities by thy power and aid. Protect O most provident Guardian of the Holy Family, the elect children of Jesus Christ ward off from us, O most loving Father, all plague of errors and depravity; be propitious to us from heaven, O most powerful Protector, in this our struggle with the powers of darkness; and as thou didst once rescue the child Jesus from the greatest peril to his life, so now defend God's holy church from the snares of the enemy and all adversity. Finally, shield every one of us with thy patronage, that, imitating thy example and strengthened by thy help, we may live a holy life, die a happy death and attain to everlasting happiness in heaven. Amen.

(300 days, once a day, Sept. 21, 1889).

Prayer to St. Joseph for Grace to Communicate Devoutly

Blessed Joseph, how sweet and wonderful a privilege was thine, not only to see, but to carry in thy arms, to kiss, and to embrace with fatherly affection, that only begotten Son of God, Whom so many kings and prophets desired to see, but were not able!

O that, inspired by thy example and aided by thy patronage, I may often with like feelings of love and reverence, embrace my Lord and Redeemer in the Blessed Sacrament of the altar, so that, when my life on earth is ended, I may merit to embrace Him eternally in heaven. Amen.

Prayer for the Month of March and Every Wednesday

Dedicate the month of March and every Wednesday to the special veneration of St. Joseph. Perform some special devotion in his honor, for which yon may say the following prayer:

O St. Joseph, who for nearly thirty years didst live in the blessed company of Jesus and of Mary, receive the humble service by which I wish to honor thee this month (day) and help me that I may also devote all the days of my life to the special service of Jesus and of Mary in trying to save the Poor Dying Sinners, and let me enjoy thy kind protection, guidance and blessing for this holy work till death. Amen.
St. Joseph, Patron of a Happy Death, pray for us and the Poor Dying Sinners. Amen.

Prayer to St. Joseph in the Form of a Rosary

In the name of the Father and of the Son and of the Holy Ghost. Amen.
O St. Joseph, best Patron of the Dying, I humbly offer thee this pious devotion of meditating on thy holy life and of praying for the Poor Dying Sinners of this day

(night). Obtain for me the grace to say these prayers with due attention and great fervor of heart, and help me that by the Precious Blood of Jesus Christ, thy Foster- son, the powerful intercession of Mary thy spouse, and thy kind fatherly protection, the Poor Dying Sinners may be saved from eternal damnation. Amen.

N. B. After every Mystery say one *Our Father* in honor of St. Joseph, as the only and best representative of God, the heavenly Father, with Whom alone he shares the beautiful name: "Father of Jesus." Then seven times the prayer "Hail, St. Joseph" (page 49) in honor of the seven Joys, Sorrows and Glories of St. Joseph. Then three times "Glory be to the Father, etc.," to thank the Blessed Trinity for all the graces and favors bestowed upon St. Joseph.

The Joyful Mysteries
(Monday and Thursday)

I. Consider the great joy of St. Joseph, when he learned from the Angel that Mary, his virgin-spouse, had conceived the Son of God to Whom he should give the name Jesus.

II. Consider the great joy of St. Joseph, when he heard

how Elizabeth had greeted Mary as the Mother of the Lord, and how Mary had chanted the beautiful hymn of praise and thanksgiving to God.

III. Consider the great joy of St. Joseph at the birth of the Savior and when he saw the Shepherds, and the Magi coming to adore the Divine Child.

IV. Consider the great joy of St. Joseph at the Presentation, when he heard Simeon foretell that the Child would be a light for the revelation of the gentiles and the glory of his people Israel.

V. Consider the great joy of St. Joseph, when after three days of sorrowful search with Mary, he found the lost Child Jesus in the Temple.

The Sorrowful Mysteries
(Tuesday and Friday)

I. Consider the great grief of St. Joseph, when- he could not solve the mystery of Mary's condition after her divine conception, and he at last resolved to leave Mary, his most beloved spouse.

II. Consider the great grief of St. Joseph, when the Savior was born like an outcast in a poor stable, and was lying in a crib and warmed by the breath of animals.

III. Consider the great grief of St. Joseph, when at the

Circumcision the new-born Savior shed his first blood for the salvation of mankind.

IV. Consider the great grief of St. Joseph when he had to flee with Mary and the Child into Egypt to save the life of the Savior from the fury of the wicked King Herod.

V. Consider the great grief of St. Joseph, when for three days in union with the sorrowful Mother Mary he sought the lost Child Jesus, his greatest treasure and consolation on earth.

The Glorious Mysteries
(Sunday, Wednesday and Saturday.)

I. Consider the great glory of St. Joseph in being chosen by God to be the spouse of Mary Immaculate, the foster-father of Jesus, and the head of the most Holy Family.

II. Consider the great glory of St. Joseph, when he saw himself for nearly thirty years loved, honored, obeyed and served by the Son of God, and when Jesus and Mary called him by the sweet name of Father.

III. Consider the great glory of St. Joseph, when he died the most happy death in the arms of Jesus and Mary who assisted and consoled him in his last moments.

IV. Consider the great glory of St. Joseph, when in Limbo he was greeted by all the Patriarchs, Prophets, and pious souls as the glorious foster-father of the Savior Who would soon redeem them.

V. Consider the great glory of St. Joseph in heaven, near the throne of Jesus and of Mary, and on earth, as the universal Patron of the Catholic Church and the best and most powerful Patron of the Dying.

At the end say three Hail Marys in memory and honor of the great part that Mary took in the Joys, Sorrows, and Glories of St. Joseph.

Closing Prayer.

dear St. Joseph! Deign to accept the humble tribute of this Rosary recited in thy honor. Obtain for me from Jesus and Mary all the graces T. need to remain faithful to thee and the cause of the Poor Dying Sinners to the end of my life, that by this devotion many Poor Dying Sinners may be saved who will then praise and thank thee in union with Jesus and Mary for all eternity. Amen.

IX. To the Lovers of St. Joseph and the Zealous Workers for the Dying

To encourage the members of the Union to remain faithful to their holy work, let them consider what the Blessed Virgin Mary revealed to the Venerable Servant of God, Mary of Agreda, concerning the privileges of St. Joseph, his great power and sanctity, and the Devotion for the Dying.

Mary of Agreda writes: "It was revealed to me that the Most High has granted St. Joseph, on account of his holiness, some privileges or prerogatives in favor of those who invoke him in a proper manner." These privileges are:

1) Through the intercession of St. Joseph a person will obtain the virtue of chastity and victory in the dangers of impure temptations.

2) Through St. Joseph a person will receive powerful graces of assistance to forsake the state of sin and to return to the friendship of God.

3) Through the mediation of St. Joseph a person will gain the favor of the Blessed Virgin Mary and a true devotion to her.

4) Through St. Joseph we shall obtain the grace of a happy death and protection against the devil at the hour

of death.

5) The evil spirits tremble when they hear the name "Joseph."

6) Through him we can obtain health of the body and help in our diverse needs.

7) His intercession will obtain for parents the grace to be blessed with children.

The Blessed Virgin said to Mary of Agreda:
"Men are not able in this life to know the sublime holiness of St. Joseph, who occupies a very high rank amongst the princes of the heavenly Jerusalem. But on the day of last judgment, the damned will bitterly weep that, on account of their sins, they did not know what a powerful means of salvation the intercession of St. Joseph is, and that they neglected to make use of it to gain the friendship of the just judge. All the children in the world are in great ignorance of the privileges and prerogatives which the Highest Lord has granted to my spouse and of the power of his intercession with the Divine Majesty and with me. I assure you that in heaven he is one of the most intimate friends of the Lord, and that he can do much to keep away the punishments of Divine Justice from the sinners. Endeavor, then, all the time of your life to increase in the devotion and hearty love of my spouse. Praise the Lord that he has so

bountifully enriched him with graces. In all your needs ask his intercession and strive to gain for him numerous clients. What my spouse asks in heaven, this the Most High will grant on earth. Great, even extraordinary graces have been surely promised to his petitions for the salvation of men."

About the Devotion for the Dying, the Blessed Virgin said:

"Not without special reason did it happen that your heart has been filled with an extraordinary compassion for the dying and with a special desire to help them in the hour of death. It is true that in that hour the souls are exposed to very great dangers arising from the evil spirits, from their own nature, and the things of this world. Death is that moment in which the acts of life are closed, and the final judgment is passed, which decides everlasting pain or perpetual glory. The Most High who gave you this desire (of helping the dying) will also grant you the grace to fulfill it indeed. I, too, confirm you in this desire, and exhort you to use all endeavors to co- operate with this grace, and to obey the Lord and me... From what I have said, you may learn how exceedingly great the danger is that death brings, and how many souls will perish in that hour in which the good merits as well as the sins begin to produce their effects. I do not tell you how many will be lost; for, if you are filled with true love for God, you would die of grief, if you would hear it. The general rule is this, that a good life is followed by a good death. Prepare your soul that you may gladly accept death, when it comes.

"In order that you may help according to your desire those who are in this extreme necessity (the Dying), I advise you to tell all to care for their soul during their life-time. Besides, every day, without exception, you must offer special prayers for this intention. Pray with a most ardent devotion of your heart to the Almighty that he may dispel the illusions by which the evil spirits deceive the dying, pray that God may destroy the snares of the devil, frustrate their wicked designs, and with His Divine Arm confound all evil spirits. You know that I have prayed in this manner for the dying, and I wish that you imitate me in this respect. You shall even command the evil spirits in the name of God to depart from the dying and not molest them. You must execute these admonitions for the love of God; I shall, then, obtain from His Majesty several privileges for you as well as for those whom you desire to help in that terrible hour. Be generous with your love, for in this matter you work not by your own power, but by the power of the Most High Who Himself wishes to work in you."

The Testimony of St. Theresa
About the Devotion to St. Joseph

St. Theresa says: "To render the Lord propitious to my prayers, I took the glorious St. Joseph for my advocate and protector, and I commended myself very earnestly to him. His help shone most clearly. This tender father of my soul, my well-beloved protector, hastened to relieve me from the languishing state I was in, just as he snatched me from greater perils of another kind, which menaced my honor and my eternal salvation. To complete my happiness, he has always heard me beyond my prayers and hopes. I do not remember having asked him anything, even to this day, that he did not grant me. What a picture I could produce, were it given me to portray the signal graces which God has heaped upon me, and the dangers corporal and spiritual from which He has delivered, me through the mediation of this blessed Saint!

"The Most High gives grace to the other saints t o help us only in such and such a need; but the glorious St. Joseph, I know by experience, has power to help us in all. Our Lord wishes to make us understand by this that, as he was submissive to St. Joseph in this land of exile, recognizing in him the authority of a foster-father and master, even so is He pleased to do his will in heaven by granting all his requests. This is what others, whom I have counselled to commend themselves to this incomparable protector, have like myself experienced. Thus the number beginning to honor him is very great, and the happy effects of his mediation confirm the truth of my words.

"Knowing today by so long experience St. Joseph's astonishing influence with God, I would wish to persuade every one to honor him with particular devotion. I have always seen those that have toward him true devotion, supported by good works, make progress in a striking manner in the spiritual advancement of souls who commend themselves to him. For the love of God, I earnestly conjure all who do not believe me, to make the trial. They will see by experience, how advantageous it is to commend themselves to this glorious Patriarch, and to honor him with particular devotion."

The "Remember" of St. Bernadine of Sienna

emember us, O blessed St. Joseph, and do not refuse us the help of thy intercession before Him Who willed to be considered thy Son. Render favorable to us, also, the Blessed Virgin

Mary, thy spouse, and the Mother of Him Who lives and reigns with the Father and the Holy Ghost forever and ever. Amen.

To the Lovers of the Poor Souls in Purgatory

Those who wish to help the Poor Souls in the best possible manner, should by making the "Heroic Act" offer the Merit of Satisfaction of all their good works and all their Indulgences for the Poor Souls. But, as a special favor, they should then ask the Poor Souls to help us in return by their prayers with God, especially in our work of saving the Dying Sinners. The Poor Souls will gladly do so, as they passed through the Agony of Death and thus know better than we what it means to be saved from hell for all eternity (Read what is said about the Heroic Act, page 17-21).

PART SECOND
OTHER DEVOTIONS AND PRAYERS FOR THE
DYING

I.
The Agony of Jesus

Those who do not wish to make the Act of Consecration and yet would like to help the dying may join the Confraternity of the Agonizing Heart of Jesus, which is under the same direction and with which the Union is intimately connected. The members of this Confraternity say every day the Daily Prayer for the Dying, and once a month on the day appointed, or on the following Sunday, pray for half an hour for the dying, which may be done by hearing Holy Mass and offering it up for them. Since the Agony of Jesus was His greatest suffering, by which Christ wished to represent the death-struggle, and to become the model, consolation and strength for the dying, the devotion and meditation of the Holy Agony of Jesus is very much, recommended to the members of the Society.

The Daily Prayer for the Dying

most merciful Jesus, lover of souls, I pray Thee by the agony of Thy most Sacred Heart and by the sorrows of Thy Immaculate Mother, cleanse in Thy Blood the sinners of the whole world, who are now in their Agony and are to die this day. Amen.

Agonizing Heart of Jesus, have mercy on the dying.

(An Indulgence of 100 days every time it If said at three distinct intervals every day during the month, a plenary Indulgence under the usual conditions. Pope Pius IX, Feb. is said with a contrite heart and devotion. 2, 1850.)

Morning and Evening Offering for the Dying

my God, for the Salvation of the Dying, especially for those who are to die this day (night), I offer to Thee through the hands of Mary Immaculate and St. Joseph, our Patron, all my thoughts, words, actions, and sufferings of this day and of my whole life, in union with the good works of our associates and pious Christians and with the merits of all the Saints in Heaven. But particularly do I thus offer to Thee for the Dying Sinners, the most Precious Blood, the bitter Passion and Death of Jesus Christ, the sorrows of His dearest Mother Mary, and all the Holy Masses that are celebrated to-day (to-night) throughout the world. I desire to renew this Act of Offering for the Dying whenever I shall say: "My Jesus, Mercy," and I promise again to consecrate my whole life to the Salvation of the Poor Dying Sinners. Give me the grace to persevere in this noble work till death. Amen.

Pious Practice for the Faithful in Their Agony

If one says, kneeling, 3 Our Fathers in remembrance of the Passion and Agony of our Lord Jesus Christ, and 3 Hail Marys, in memory of the bitter sorrows experienced by our Lady at the foot of the Cross during the Agony of her Divine Son, for the faithful in their Agony, he gains each time an Indulgence of 300 days, and if said once a day during a month a plenary Indulgence under the usual conditions.

(Pope Pius VII, April 18, 1809)

Meditation on the Agony of Jesus
(For the Hour of Intercession for Dying).

"Jesus knowing that His hour was come, that He should go out of this world to the Father, having loved His own who were in the world, He loved them unto the end."

By these words St. John describes the infinite love that was burning in the Heart of Jesus the night before His Passion. This infinite love moved Him to institute the Blessed Sacrament, "the memorial of His love," to deliver that beautiful discourse ("Love one another as I loved you"), and that fervent prayer in which he asked his Heavenly Father: "That the love wherewith Thou hast loved me, may be in them and I in them." He then goes to the Garden of Olives to begin His Passion. To make Jesus, so to speak, fully understand and feel the cause, the extent, and the effects of His bitter Passion and Death, God sends to him that terrible suffering which caused His Agony so that "His sweat became as drops of blood trickling down upon the ground." Consider now, briefly, the causes of this greatest of our Savior's sufferings.

I. Christ is loaded with the sins of all men so that he appears before the Divine Majesty as the greatest malefactor. If you now consider how great a horror Jesus feels even of the smallest sin, how much must it then grieve and oppress His Heart to see the Infinite Majesty so much offended and outraged by most ungrateful creatures, and Himself loaded with all their sins and crimes.

II. Then Almighty God shows Jesus all the sufferings that our Divine Savior afterwards took upon Himself for the sins and crimes of all men. This sight has the effect of causing Jesus to feel and suffer all at once in His Heart whatever He had to suffer afterwards in His Holy Body by being scourged, crowned with thorns, etc. His human nature shudders at the thought of so cruel sufferings and so ignominious a death.

III. But God also shows Him the effect of His bitter Passion and Death: that the honor of the Most High would be restored, the Divine Justice be appeased, mankind be reconciled to God, and a number of souls be eternally saved, namely, all those that would strive to profit by His Passion and Death. But, at the same time, Christ also foresees that, notwithstanding all His sufferings, a great many will despise His love, even abuse and profane His Sacred Blood, and on that account, be condemned to eternal hell-fire. This foresight greatly increases His Sufferings and He begins to become very sorrowful even unto death.

IV. There arises now in the Heart of Jesus the greatest struggle between His Infinite Love for the salvation of all men and the Infinite Justice of the Divine Nature demanding the eternal reprobation of impenitent sinners. Christ's infinite Love wishes to save all men, as He is also willing to suffer and die for all. Therefore, He begins to pray and ask His Heavenly Father: "My Father, if it be possible, let this chalice pass from me." This longing and struggling for the salvation of souls brings Jesus into a state of so great an agony that it even presses the Blood from the pores of His Body. "His sweat becomes as drops of blood, trickling down upon the ground."

This same desire for the salvation of poor sinners makes Jesus also exclaim in His Agony on the Cross:

"My God, my God, why hast Thou forsaken me?" by which words, according to the revelations made to Ven. Mary of Agreda, Jesus principally complains of being forsaken, by so many souls that He wishes to save by His Death, but that reject His Love to their greater eternal damnation. And to express how much even at the moment of His death He longs for their salvation, he again exclaims, "I thirst," that means: I am consumed by the most ardent desire for the possession of these immortal souls.

V. Now consider that all the sins come from the heart and will of man and, therefore, Christ principally suffers in His Heart to atone for our many interior sins. Will you not then begin to hate and avoid sin? Do you not feel sorry for the many sins of your past life? Do you not also wish to save immortal souls and to comfort Jesus in His Agony as the Angel strengthens Him in the garden of Olives? But Jesus says to you: "As long as you did it to one of these my brethren, you did it to me." When you clothed your neighbor, you clothed your Saviour. Therefore, hasten to assist, to comfort, to save the dying, and you will comfort your Agonizing Savior, you will even struggle with Him for the salvation of immortal souls. Thank Jesus then, for the Agony He suffered for you and all poor sinners, and promise Him to show your gratitude by serving him in the Dying Sinners, that they may be saved for all eternity.

Litany of Jesus in the Garden of Olives

Lord, *have mercy on us.*
Christ, *have mercy on us.*
Lord, *have mercy on us.*
Christ, *hear us.*
Christ, *graciously hear us.*
God, the Father of Heaven, *have mercy on us.*
God, the Son, Redeemer of the world, *have mercy on us.*
God, the Holy Ghost, *have mercy on us.*
Holy Trinity, one God, *have mercy on us.*
Jesus, Who didst go to a solitary place to pray before delivering Thyself up to Thine enemies, *have mercy on the Dying.*
Jesus, Whose heart was oppressed by mortal sadness in the Garden of Gethsemani, *have mercy on the Dying.*
Jesus, filled with fear at the thought of the torments of Thy Passion and at our sins, have mercy on the Dying.
Jesus overwhelmed with sadness by forseeing the fruitlessness of Thy suffering for souls that refuse to profit by them, *have mercy on the Dying.*
Jesus, strengthened in Thine Agony by an Angel from Heaven, *have mercy on the Dying.*
Jesus, accepting the chalice of Thy Passion for love of us, *have mercy on the Dying.*
Jesus, Who didst say in the midst of Thine anguish:

"Father, not My will, but Thine be done," *have mercy on the Dying.*

Jesus, persevering in prayer, notwithstanding the weakness of nature, *have mercy on the Dying.*

Jesus, Who didst come to Thine Apostles and find them sleeping, *have mercy on the Dying.*

Jesus, Who didst say to them: "Could you not watch with me one hour?" *have mercy on the Dying.*

Lamb of God, Who takest away the sins of the world, *spare us, O Lord.*

Lamb of God, Who takest away the sins of the world, *graciously hear us, O Lord.*

Lamb of God, Who takest away the sins of the world, *have mercy on us, O Lord.*

V. Agonizing Heart of Jesus.

R. Have mercy on the Dying.

Let us Pray:

my Divine Savior, remember the sadness of Heart which oppressed Thee, and the fear which Thou hast felt when, being in Agony, Thou didst pray the longer and water the earth with a Sweat of Blood. I offer to Thee with tender love, and I beseech Thee, by every drop of that Precious

Blood, to have mercy on the Dying, and to put away all their sins. Amen.

Prayer for the Dying

Lord Jesus Christ we beseech Thee, by Thy bitter Agony and prayer in the garden, that Thou wouldst be pleased to be an advocate with Thy eternal Father on behalf of these Thy servants: lay before Him all those drops of blood which, in Thy anguish of spirit, flowed from Thy body, and offer, them for the remission of all their sins: that in this hour of extremity they may be discharged -from that handwriting of sin which stands against them, and from that punishment which they fear to be too justly due to their sins.

Our Father, Hail, Mary.

Lord Jesus Christ! who for our salvation was pleased to suffer death on the cross, we beseech Thee to offer all the anguish and pains Thou didst then endure, and most especially at the hour of Thy death, in behalf of these Thy servants that they may be accepted in their favor, for the good of their souls, for the obtaining of a happy hour, and for the release from that punishment which they have deserved for their sins.

Our Father, Hail, Mary.

Lord Jesus Christ! who hadst such a boundless love for man as to induce Thee to become man for his salvation, we beseech Thee to let this, Thy infinite charity and goodness towards mankind, so plead in behalf of these Thy poor servants, that by Thy powerful mediation their soul, at the moment of its departure from the body, being freed from the bonds of sin, may find a full admittance through the gate that lead to the mansions of eternal bliss.

Our Father, Hail, Mary.

Lord Jesus Christ! who by Thy precious blood has redeemed us, we beseech Thee to imprint deep in the soul of these Thy servants, the memory of Thy most sacred wounds, that, having them perpetually in sight they may be encouraged to suffer with patience and resignation, and be armed against all the pangs of death. Let them cheerfully submit to all the difficulties of their condition, and begin, even here, to be united to Thee with a love that shall never end. Grant them now to partake of the fruit of Thy incarnation, of Thy bitter passion, of Thy glorious resurrection and admirable ascension. Grant that they may be sensible of the effects of Thy holy mysteries and sacraments, and of all the prayers which are offered by the whole church.

Remember, O Lord, that Thou wert once in the straits of death; and in this extremity, after crying out to Thy eternal Father, and commending Thy spirit to Him didst expire. Behold now these Thy servants in their anguish crying aloud to Thee; stand Thou by them, defend and comfort them in this their distress, and receive their soul into Thy merciful embrace.

Remember, O Jesus, that Thy arms were stretched forth, Thy side opened, and Thy sacred head bowed down from the cross; have regard now, we beseech Thee, for the souls of these Thy servants, which, departing out of this world, seek refuge in Thee; receive them into Thy arms, clasp them to Thy breast, and there let them hide themselves, secure from the attacks of all their enemies, until the anger of God pass over. Into Thy hand we commend their spirit, which has been created and redeemed by Thee; despise not, we beseech Thee, the work of Thy hands.

O Christ Jesus, who wast crucified for our redemption, we beseech Thee, by that love which brought Thee from heaven, to have compassion on the soul of Thy servants; forgive them all their sins, and by the merits of Thy bitter passion, satisfy for all their failings and supply their defects; let them now experience the multitude of Thy tender mercies, and be sensible how good Thou, O Lord, art. Dispose now their soul by Thy grace, so that they may be prepared at Thy call to go forth to meet Thee, their heavenly bridegroom. Grant them, we beseech Thee, true patience and perfect resignation in their pain and anguish. Give them full discharge from all their sins, confirm their faith; strengthen their hope and perfect their charity, that, departing hence, their souls many be received into Thy mercy. O dear Redeemer, by that distress which Thou didst suffer on the cross when Thou didst cry out to Thy eternal Father, we pray Thee to show mercy to these Thy servants in their extremity; hear the sighs and desires of their heart; and since they are now deprived of their faculty of speech, speak Thou for them, we beseech Thee, who are the eternal word, and to whom the Father will refuse nothing.

By Thy victory over death, and the infinite merits of Thy passion, we beseech Thee, on behalf of these servants, to have no other thoughts than of peace, of mercy and comfort, and not of affliction. Bear them up against all distrust and despair; deliver them from their necessities, and be their comforter in their distress. Let those hands which were once nailed to the cross now plead for them, and obtaining their pardon, conduct them to eternal rest. Amen.

II.
The Precious Blood of Jesus Christ

St. Paul attributes the remission of sins, the grace of our redemption, and our eternal Salvation principally to the Most Precious Blood of Christ. St. John says: "The Blood of Jesus Christ cleanses us from all sin." It is therefore a very useful devotion to offer up the Most Precious Blood of Christ for the Poor Dying Sinners. Especially at the Consecration and Elevation of the chalice in Holy Mass, this offering of the Precious Blood should prove very efficacious for the Dying. For, when the priest consecrates the Blood of Christ in Holy Mass, he says: "This is the chalice of my Blood, of the new and eternal testament, a mystery of faith, which shall be shed for you and for many unto the remission of sins." May the word "Many" in this formula of Consecration signify the Many Dying Sinners of that hour and day.

Nine Offerings of the Precious Blood for the Dying

I.

Jesus, with our dear Mother, Mary-Immaculate, we adore and offer up for the Dying Sinners all Thy Sacred Blood shed at Thy Circumcision, when Thou didst receive the sweet name Jesus. By this Thy Precious Blood and Thy Most Holy Name, we ask Thee to forgive the Dying all sins committed against faith. Grant to all Dying Children the grace of holy Baptism and to the rest of the Dying the light of the true, saving faith. Amen.

Our Father. Hail Mary. Glory be to the Father.

We pray Thee, therefore, to help Thy servants,
Whom Thou hast redeemed by Thy Precious Blood. My Jesus mercy. Amen.

II.

O Jesus, with our dear Mother, Mary Immaculate, we adore and offer up for the Dying Sinners all Thy Sacred Blood which trickled down at Thy Holy Agony in the garden of Olives. By this Thy Precious Blood and Thy Holy Agony we ask Thee to forgive the Dying all their sins of ingratitude. Grant them the grace to make a sacrifice of their life and to die with full resignation to

the will of Thy Heavenly Father. Amen.
Our Father. Hail Mary, Glory be to the Father.

We pray Thee, therefore to help Thy servants.
Whom Thou hast redeemed by Thy Precious Blood. My Jesus Mercy. Amen.

III.

O Jesus, with our dear Mother, Mary Immaculate, we adore and offer up for the Dying Sinners all Thy Sacred Blood shed at the most cruel scourging at the pillar. By this Thy Precious Blood and all the wounds of Thy mangled body we ask Thee to forgive the Dying all their sins of impurity and to clothe their souls with the beautiful garment of sanctifying grace and of holy purity. Amen.
Our Father. Hail Mary. Glory be to the Father.

We pray Thee, therefore, to help Thy servants,
Whom Thou hast redeemed by Thy Precious Blood. My Jesus, mercy. Amen.

IV.

O Jesus, with our dear Mother, Mary Immaculate, we adore and offer up for the Dying Sinners all Thy Sacred Blood pressed out of Thy Sacred Head by the horrible

crown of thorns. By this Thy Precious Blood and the sufferings of The Sacred Head we ask Thee to forgive the Dying all their interior sins committed in thought and desire, especially by pride. Grant them true humility that they may ask for pardon and mercy. Amen.
Our Father. Hail Mary. Glory be to the Father.

We pray Thee, therefore, to help Thy servants, Whom Thou hast redeemed by Thy Precious Blood. My Jesus, mercy. Amen.

V.

O Jesus, with our dear Mother, Mary Immaculate, we adore and offer up for the Dying Sinners all Thy Sacred Blood shed when carrying the heavy Cross and falling so often under its weight. By this Thy Precious Blood and the sufferings of Thy repeated falls we ask Thee to forgive the Dying their repeated relapses into sin. Grant them the grace to carry their cross with patience as atonement for their many sins. Amen.
Our Father. Hail Mary. Glory be to the Father.

We pray Thee, therefore, to help Thy servants, Whom Thou hast redeemed by Thy Precious Blood. My Jesus, mercy. Amen.

VI.

O Jesus, with our dear Mother, Mary Immaculate, we adore and offer up for the Dying Sinners all Thy Sacred Blood that gushed forth from Thy Sacred Hands and Feet when being nailed to the Cross. By this Thy Precious Blood and the wounds of Thy Sacred Hands and Feet we ask Thee to forgive the Dying all their exterior sins committed by any bad actions. Unite them now to Thy holy Cross that they may suffer in the spirit of true penance. Amen.
Our Father. Hail Mary. Glory be to the Father.

We pray Thee, therefore, to help Thy servants,
Whom Thou hast redeemed by Thy Precious Blood. My Jesus, mercy. Amen.

VII.

O Jesus, with our dear Mother, Mary Immaculate, we adore and offer up for the Dying Sinners all Thy Sacred Blood that was flowing from all the wounds of Thy Holy Body when hanging on the Cross. By this Thy Precious Blood and Thy most Holy Death we ask Thee to forgive the Dying all sins committed against hope. Let them not despair, give them full confidence in the merits of Thy bitter Passion and Death and assist them at the last moment that they may die a truly happy

death. Amen.
Our Father. Hail Mary. Glory be to the Father.

We pray Thee, therefore, to help Thy servants,
Whom Thou hast redeemed by Thy Precious Blood. My
Jesus, mercy. Amen.

VII.

O Jesus, with our dear Mother, Mary Immaculate, we
adore and offer up for the Dying Sinners all Thy Sacred
Blood that came forth from Thy Sacred Heart when
pierced with a lance. By this Thy Precious Blood and
the love of Thy Sacred Heart we ask Thee to forgive the
Dying all their sins of neglect, and after purifying their
hearts in Thy Precious Blood to enkindle in them the
fire of Thy Divine Love, so pleasing to Thy Heavenly
Father.
Amen.
Our Father. Hail Mary. Glory be to the Father.
We pray Thee, therefore, to help Thy servants,
Whom Thou hast redeemed by Thy Precious Blood. My
Jesus, mercy. Amen.

IX.

O Jesus with   our dear Mother, Mary Immaculate, we
adore and offer up for the Dying Sinners all Thy Sacred

Blood that is daily flowing on all our altars in all the Holy Masses for the remission of sins. By this Thy Precious Blood and Thy great love for man in the Blessed Sacrament we ask Thee to forgive the Dying all sins committed against Thee in the Holy Eucharist. From this most Holy Sacrament plead now, O Jesus, with Thy Holy Body and Blood and Thy Holy Wounds for all the Dying Sinners that they receive from Thy infinite mercy the grace of final perseverance, and thus be saved forever. Amen.
Our Father. Hail Mary. Glory be to the Father.

We pray Thee, therefore, to help Thy servants,
Whom Thou hast redeemed by Thy Precious Blood. My Jesus, mercy. Amen.

The Sacrifice of Holy Mass for the Dying Sinners

There is no better means of assisting the Dying than to have Holy Masses said and offered for the Dying. Whenever, therefore your means allow it, show that you have, indeed, true love for your dying neighbor. At least, often assist at Holy Mass with the intention of offering it up for them. Accustom yourself then, to make acts of adoration, atonement, thanksgiving, and petition for them and, as it were, in their stead. Particularly, at the moment of Consecration, offer up with all fervor the most Holy Body and Blood of Jesus Christ to His Heavenly Father that He may apply to the souls of the Dying the merits of Christ's redemption.

Prayers at Mass for the Dying

I. Before Mass

O, my Jesus, I firmly believe that the Sacrifice of Mass is the renewal of that great sacrifice which Thou didst offer at the Last Supper and on the Cross for the salvation of the world. Grant me the grace to assist at it with due attention and devotion, in union with Thy sorrowful Mother, standing under the Cross. Through the hands of Mary, Thy Immaculate Mother, I wish to offer this and all other holy Masses that are celebrated today all over the world for the eternal salvation of the Dying Sinners, the deliverance of the poor souls in purgatory, and the welfare of this house, and of all those for whom I am bound and Thou wishest me to pray. My Jesus, Mercy. Amen.

II At the Beginning of Mass

O, my God, with all the angels and saints, I humbly adore Thee, most Holy Trinity, Father, Son, and Holy Ghost, and in order to give due honor to Thy divine majesty, I offer up through my Mother Mary, all the praise and homage which Jesus Christ, Thy beloved Son, in whom Thou art well pleased, did offer in his mortal life, and is still offering in this most holy sacrifice. Honor, praise, and adoration, now and forever to Thy most Holy Name, through Jesus Christ, Thy Son, our Lord and Saviour. Mayest Thou be also glorified by the Salvation of the Poor Dying Sinners that they may praise with us Thy infinite mercy for all eternity. My Jesus Mercy. Amen.

III. At the Offertory

Almighty and eternal God, I offer Thee through the hands of the priest and my Immaculate Mother Mary, this bread and wine in union with my body and soul and all I have that it may become a most pleasing sacrifice to Thy divine majesty. In order to render Thee due thanksgiving, I offer up all the thanks that Thy divine Son gives to Thee in this August sacrifice for all the benefits, graces and favors bestowed upon me and all mankind, but especially upon the Dying Sinners that their ingratitude may not hinder the grace of true conversion. What thanks will they offer Thee for all eternity, if like the penitent thief they will hear the consoling words: "This day thou shalt be with me in paradise." My Jesus, Mercy. Amen.

IV. After the Consecration

O Jesus, my Saviour, I firmly believe that Thou art now present upon the altar, with Thy body and soul, Thy flesh and blood, Thy humanity and divinity. I most profoundly adore Thee with all the holy angels that invisibly surround Thy altar. Thou now renewest the great sacrifice of the Cross. Through the hands of Mary, Thy Immaculate Mother, I offer up this Thy sacred body and Thy most holy blood, as atonement for my many sins, and those of the whole world, but especially for the Poor Dying Sinners. Plead Thou, O Jesus, for them, with Thy blood, and Thy most holy wounds, at the throne of Thy merciful Father! May Thy body preserve their souls to life everlasting, and Thy blood again be shed, for the remission of their sins, that Thou didst not suffer and die in vain for them. My Jesus, Mercy. Amen.

V. At the Communion

O Jesus, I am not worthy that Thou shouldst enter into my soul, but speak one word, and my soul shall be healed. How I long to receive Thee now into my heart, as Thy Holy Church wishes me to communicate even daily. Come then into my heart with all Thy graces and blessings! Unite me most intimately with Thy Sacred Heart, preserve me from sin, let me always fulfil Thy holy will, for Thy greater honor and glory, and give me the grace of final perseverance. I now recommend to Thee my parents, teachers, friends, and enemies, but especially the Dying Sinners, that through the graces of this sacrifice they may die united with Thee and strengthened by Thy holy blessing. Let also the poor souls share in the merits of this sacrifice! O Mary, present these petitions to Thy divine Son, that we all may find grace and salvation. Amen.

III.
The Reception of Holy Communion for the Dying Sinners

There is no holier act and no greater honor for us mortals than to receive Jesus Christ into our own heart in Holy Communion. Our prayer is never more pleasing to God and never more efficacious than when united with the prayer of Jesus really present in our soul. In Holy Communion Jesus becomes our own personal gift. What better sacrifice could we personally offer to the Divine Majesty from the altar of our own heart for the Poor Dying Sinners than the Dear Jesus with the five holy wounds of His Sacred Body and the most Precious Blood of His Loving Heart! Let then all the members of this Union try their very best frequently, and, if possible, even daily to receive Holy Communion. Do not deprive the Dying of this best help that you can give them by your daily Communion in connection with Holy Mass. Ask your Immaculate Mother Mary and your special Patron St. Joseph to help you in your preparation and thanksgiving, for they carried the same Infant Jesus in their hands and pressed Him to their hearts. During the blessed moments that Jesus is really present in your soul, ask Him most fervently by His ardent desire for the Salvation of souls to spare and to save the Poor Dying Sinners.

Pious Acts Before Receiving Holy Communion

O Jesus, I firmly believe that Thou, the Son of God, and of My Mother, Mary Immaculate, art really present in the Sacred Host. Prostrate on my knees, I most humbly adore Thee with all the Holy Angels that invisibly surround Thy altar. I thank Thee for this holy Catholic faith in which I wish to live and die. O Jesus, I most confidently hope that Thou wilt come now into my heart with all Thy graces and blessings. How much do I need them for myself and for the Poor Dying Sinners! O Jesus, if I now consider Thy Infinite Majesty and the nothingness and sinfulness of my low human nature, I must confess that I am really not worthy that Thou shouldst come to me. Thou alone canst make me worthy. Speak, then, one word of Thy almighty power, purify my soul in Thy most Precious Blood, and my soul shall be healed. Thou wilt surely grant this my request, for I know that Thou lovest me. Love for man brings Thee from heaven upon the altar, but love for me bring Thee from the altar into my heart. What else could I now offer Thee, but the best love of my own heart and the pure, beautiful love of Mary and St. Joseph. This love for Thee, O Jesus, fills my heart with the most ardent desire to receive Thee. Come, then, O Jesus! All I am and all I have shall be Thine. I will only belong to Thee. Take full possession of my heart. Erect in it the throne of Thy grace, of Thy love, and of Thy mercy for me and all the Poor Dying Sinners. Amen.

Prayer After Holy Communion

O Jesus, I firmly believe that Thou, the Son of God, and of my Mother, Mary Immaculate, didst come into my heart. With most profound humility, I wish to honor, praise, love, and adore Thee, as Thy Mother Mary and St. Joseph loved and adored Thee, when lying in the crib. Prom the bottom of my heart I thank Thee for this Holy Communion and all the graces and blessings Thou didst bring to my soul. In return for Thy love I wish to make now a complete sacrifice of myself to Thee, through Mary, Thy and my Immaculate Mother. All that I am, all I have, and all I do, shall belong only to Thee! O Jesus, keep the thought of Thy holy presence before my mind that I may never offend Thee by sin. O Jesus, hear my prayer, save the Dying Sinners, console the poor souls in purgatory, keep me pure in body and soul, and give now the fullness of Thy blessing both to me and all those whom I have recommended to Thy loving Hear. My Jesus, Mercy. Amen.

IV. The Visit and Adoration of the Blessed Sacrament

The center of all real Catholic devotion should be the Blessed Sacrament. For this reason, the members of the Union and Society for the Dying should love to visit and adore the most Holy Sacrament. There you find the loving Savior, the real Sacred Heart, the most Precious Blood, and an abundance of graces that Christ is ready to distribute to his faithful adorers for their own welfare and the Salvation of those they wish to save. At the foot of the Tabernacle is the best place for prayer, for there you plead with Christ, Who is continually interceding for man in the Sacrament of love and only waiting for heroic souls that wish to become like unto him, namely, another Savior for the Poor Dying Sinners. Help to promote, as far as lies in your power, the great Eucharistic movement of our days. Try to be a daily communicant and to attend the Holy Hour where it is kept. If you, are a Tertiary, or a child of St. Francis, consider that our holy Father St. Francis often spent entire hours, especially at night, before the Tabernacle to plead for the poor sinners, and when Christ appeared to him in the chapel of the Portiuncula, and told him to ask a favor of Him, St. Francis would only ask: "Pardon for the poor sinners." The great Portiuncula Indulgence was not asked by St. Francis for the poor souls in purgatory, but for the poor sinners here on earth. Before the Tabernacle, you will then, as it were, storm the Sacred Heart and the throne of Mercy, and obtain the greatest victories over satan and hell for the Poor Dying Sinners.

Accustom yourself, when entering or leaving the church or chapel to say; "Honor, Praise and Adoration without end, to Jesus Christ in the most Holy Sacrament. O Sacrament most holy, O Sacrament divine, all Praise and all Thanksgiving be every moment Thine. "

The beautiful prayer of St. Francis was:

"We adore Thee, most Holy Lord, Jesus Christ, here and in all Thy churches that are in the whole world, and we give The praise, because by Thy Holy Cross Thou hast redeemed the world."

At the time of Adoration you may say the Rosary of the Blessed Sacrament for the Dying in this manner.

Add after the word Jesus in the Hail Mary: "Praised and adored in the most Holy Sacrament of the Altar, ... Now and forever more, ... Holy Mary ..."

After each decade insert the Daily Prayer for the Dying: "I promise to Almighty God ..." (page 8).

Acts of Adoration and Petitions for the Dying Sinners.
(For the Holy Hour)

1) O Jesus, I firmly believe that Thou are really present in the most Holy Sacrifice of the Altar, and I heartily thank Thee for the gift of the Holy Catholic faith which makes me enjoy the blessings of Thy Holy Presence. With Mary Immaculate, St. Joseph, and all the holy Angels and Saints I wish to adore Thee, my Lord and my God. Accept now my fervent prayers which I offer Thee for the thousands of little children that are in danger of dying without holy baptism. O Jesus, I offer Thee all the merits of Thy Holy Incarnation, Miraculous Birth, Divine Infancy and Happy Childhood for the Dying Children that they all may receive the grace of holy baptism and die as the best children of Thy heavenly Father. Preserve also, O good Jesus, the purity and innocence of the good children from the corruption of the terrible vice of impurity and let no child die in the sad state of mortal sin. Amen. Let us pray for all the Dying Children: *Our Father ... Hail Mary ... Glory be to the Father.*

O Jesus, I confidently hope to receive for myself and all others all the graces Thou hast promised us in this most Holy Sacrament of the Altar. With Mary Immaculate, St.

Joseph, and all the holy Angels and Saints, I wish to adore Thee, my greatest Benefactor and best Hope of Salvation. Accept now my fervent prayers which I offer Thee for the thousands of Dying Pagans who do not even know or honor the one true God. O Jesus, Who art the Light of the World, enlighten these poor Dying Pagans and make them clearly see that there is but one true God Who is their Creator and last end. O Jesus, Thou, the Savior of all mankind, help now by a special grace these Poor Dying Pagans that being enlightened and moved they may turn to the one true God with perfect love and sincere contrition for all their sins and thus be saved. Amen Let us pray for the Dying Pagans: *Our Father . . .* as above.

O Jesus, with my whole heart I love Thee in the most Holy Sacrament of the Altar. Help me to love Thee more and more to the end of my life. With Mary Immaculate, St. Joseph, and all the holy Angels, and Saints I wish to adore Thee, the infinite Beauty and Love. Accept now my fervent prayers that I offer Thee for all the Dying Jews, Muslims, and Infidels. May Thy Precious Blood now plead for Mercy and Thy bitter Passion and Death obtain for them special graces of conversion that they may see that Thou art their loving Savior and Redeemer. From this Holy Sacrament plead again with Thy holy wounds at the throne of Thy merciful Father. "Father, forgive them, they do not know what they do." Convert them like the penitent thief that they may also hear the consoling words: "This day thou shalt be with me in paradise." Amen. Let us pray for the Dying Jews, Muslims, and infidels: *Our Father* ... as above.

O Jesus, I heartily long for Thee in the Most Holy Sacrament, the greatest treasure of my soul. With Mary Immaculate, St. Joseph, and all the holy Angels and Saints, I wish to adore Thee, my Highest Good and best Friend. Accept now my fervent prayers which I offer Thee for all the Dying Heretics and Schismatics. Unite them now at least spiritually to Thy Holy Catholic Church. Be Thou now the good Shepherd even of those who are not of Thy fold, and let them partake of the graces of Thy Holy Church that they may die either as children of Thy Church, or at least in good faith with an act of Perfect Contrition for their sins. I offer up Thy most Precious Blood in atonement for all they may have said or done against Thy Holy Church, against Thee in the Blessed Sacrament, and against Thy Holy Mother Mary. Amen. Let us pray for all the Dying Heretics and Schismatics: *Our Father* ... as above.

O Jesus, I offer myself entirely to Thee in the Most Holy Sacrament of the Altar, Thou the King of my heart. With Mary Immaculate, St. Joseph, and all the holy

Angels and Saints, I specially adore Thy most Sacred Heart, present in the Holy Sacrament. Accept now my fervent prayers for the Salvation of all Dying Catholics that they may die well prepared by the Holy Sacraments, especially by the worthy reception of the Viaticum. May the reception of Thy most Holy Body defend them against the evil spirit, and lead their departing soul to life everlasting. Let this Holy Sacrament be the best pledge of their glorious resurrection and eternal happiness in heaven. I specially recommend to Thee those whom Thou wilt call next from our midst or our family that by the mercy of Thy Sacred Heart none may be lost. Amen. Let us pray for all Dying Catholics: Our Father ... as above.

O Jesus, I consecrate myself entirely to Thy Purest Love in the Most Holy Sacrament of the Altar, the best proof and most glorious crown on Thy Infinite Kindness, Love, and Mercy for Thy special friends. With Mary Immaculate, St. Joseph, and all the Holy Angels and Saints, I wish to adore most lovingly Thy Thorn-crowned Head and Thy Holy Face, which Thy ministering Angels always behold and honor in this most Blessed Sacrament. Accept now my fervent prayers for a Happy Death for all Dying Priests and Dying Religious, so dear to Thy Loving Heart, that they all may die as the best images of Thy Divine Person, and of Thy most Holy Life. May the Priests of Thy Holy Catholic Church like St. Joseph take the best care of Thy Most Holy Body in the Blessed Sacrament and thus shine as the most glorious crown encircling the Head of Thy Mystical Body, the Church. May the Religious, who are specially consecrated to Thy Purest Love, always excel in their fervent devotion to the Blessed Sacrament that they best reflect Thy Most Holy Face in Thy spotless Bride, Thy Pure Holy Church. Let all the Priests and Religious die like St. Joseph in Thy loving embrace and in the arms of Thy dearest Mother Mary. Amen. Let us pray for all the Dying Priests and Religious: Our Father. . . as above.

The Devotion to the Most Holy Name

In our struggle with the powers of hell for the Salvation of the Dying, let us not forget nor neglect the beautiful devotion to the Most Holy Name of Jesus. "There is no other name under heaven given to men whereby we must be saved," says St. Peter. This devotion was especially propagated by the two Franciscan Missionaries, St. Bernardine of Sienna, the Standard-bearer of the Holy Name, and St. John Capistran, who by the power of this Holy Name obtained for the Christians one of the most glorious victories over the enemies of our holy religion. Let us, then, often piously call upon the Holy Name of Jesus and apply its wonderful power to the souls of the Dying by praying with all fervor: "My Jesus, Mercy on the Poor Dying Sinners! Sweetest Jesus, be not to them a Judge, but a Savior! Give them the grace to expire devoutly invoking Thy Most Holy Name that this Holy Name and the sweet Name of Mary and Joseph on their lips and in their hearts may drive away the devil and procure their eternal Salvation.

Litany of the Holy Name of Jesus

Lord, *have mercy on us.*
Christ, *have mercy on us.*
Lord, *have mercy on us.*
Christ, *hear us.*
Christ, *graciously hear us.*
God, the Father of heaven, — *have mercy on us.*
God, the Son, Redeemer of the world,—*have mercy on us.*
God, the Holy Ghost,—*have mercy on us.*
Holy Trinity, one God,—*have mercy on us.*
Jesus, Son of the living God,   —   *have mercy on us.*
Jesus, splendor of the Father,
Jesus, brightness of eternal light,
Jesus, king of glory,
Jesus, son of justice,

Jesus, Son of the Virgin Mary,   *Have mercy on us*
Jesus, most amiable,
Jesus, most admirable,
Jesus, powerful God,
Jesus, Father of the world to come,
Jesus, Angel of the great Council,
Jesus, most powerful,
Jesus, most patient,
Jesus, most obedient,
Jesus, meek and humble of heart,
Jesus, lover of chastity,
Jesus, God of peace,
Jesus, lover of mankind,
Jesus, author of life,
Jesus, model of virtues,
Jesus, zealous for souls,
Jesus, our God,
Jesus, our refuge,
Jesus, Father of the poor,
Jesus, treasure of the faithful,
Jesus, good shepherd,
Jesus, true light,
Jesus, eternal wisdom,
Jesus, infinite goodness,
Jesus, our Way and our Life,
Jesus, joy of angels,

Jesus, king of patriarchs,
Jesus, master of the apostles,
Jesus, teacher of the evangelists,
Jesus, strength of martyrs,
Jesus, light of confessors,
Jesus, purity of virgins,
Jesus, crown of all saints,

Be merciful unto us,—*Spare us, O Jesus!*
Be merciful unto us,—*Hear us O Jesus!*
From all evil,—*Deliver us, O Jesus!*
From all sin,   —   *Deliver us, O Jesus!*
From Thy wrath,
From the snares of the devil,
From the spirit of uncleanliness,
From eternal death,
From the neglect of Thy inspirations,
Through the mystery of Thy Incarnation,
Through Thy nativity,
Through Thy childhood,
Through. Thy most sacred life,
Through Thy labors,
Through Thy agony and passion,
Through Thy death and burial,
Through Thy resurrection,
Through Thy ascension,

Through Thy institution of the Most Holy Eucharist,
Through Thy joys,
Through Thy glory,

Lamb of God, Who takest away the sins of the world,—*Spare us, O Jesus.*
Lamb of God, Who takest away the sins of the world,—*Hear us, O Jesus.*
Lamb of God, Who takest away the sins of the world,—*Have mercy on us, O Jesus.*
Jesus, *hear us.* Jesus *graciously hear us.*

Let us pray:

O Lord, Jesus Christ! Who hast said: Ask, and ye shall receive; seek, and ye shall find; knock, and it shall be opened unto you; mercifully attend to our supplications, and grant us the divine gift of Thy charity, that we may love Thee with our whole heart and never desist from Thy praise. Grant, O Lord, that we may have a perpetual fear and love of Thy Holy Name, for Thou never failest to direct and govern those whom Thou instructest in Thy true and solid love, Who livest and reignest world without end. Amen.

The Devotion to the Sacred Heart of Jesus for the Dying

Among the great favors our Lord promised the Blessed Margaret Mary Alaçoque for those who foster a special devotion to His Sacred Heart are also some which are very consoling for the poor sinners, especially at the hour of death. Our Lord said: "I will be their refuge during life, and especially in the hour of death." "Sinners shall find in my heart a fountain and boundless ocean of mercy." "I will give priests the power of touching the hardest hearts." Offer then your devotion of the first Friday of the month for the Dying Sinners that the merciful Heart of Jesus may also be to them a fountain and boundless ocean of mercy.

Act of Consecration to the Sacred Heart of Jesus
(Leo XIII. May 25, 1899)

ost sweet Jesus, Redeemer of the human race, look down upon us, humbly prostrate before Thy altar. We are Thine and Thine we wish to be; but to be more surely united with Thee, behold each one of us freely consecrates himself today to Thy Most Sacred Heart. Many indeed have never know Thee; many, too, despising Thy precepts, have rejected Thee. Have mercy on them all, most merciful Jesus, and draw them to Thy Sacred Heart. Be Thou King, O Lord, not only of the faithful who have never forsaken Thee, but also of the prodigal children who have abandoned Thee; grant that they may quickly return to their Father's house, lest they die of wretchedness and hunger. Be Thou King of those who are deceived by erroneous opinions or whom discord keeps aloof, and call them back to the harbor of truth and unity of faith, so that soon there may be but one flock and one shepherd. Be Thou King of all those who are still involved in the darkness of idolatry or of Islamism, and refuse not to draw them all into the light and kingdom of God. Turn Thy eyes of mercy toward the children of that race, once Thy chosen people. Of old they called down upon themselves the Blood of the Saviour; may it now descend upon them a laver of redemption and of life. Grant, O Lord, to Thy Church assurance of freedom and immunity from harm; give peace and order to all nations, and make the earth resound from pole to pole with one cry: Praise to the Divine Heart that wrought our salvation to It be glory and honor forever. Amen.

Litany of the Sacred Heart

Lord, *have mercy on us.*
Christ, *have mercy on us.*
Lord, *have mercy on us.*
Christ, *hear us.*
Christ, *graciously hear us.*
God, the Father of heaven, — *have mercy on us.*
God, the Son Redeemer of the world,
God, the Holy Ghost.
Holy Trinity, one God,
Heart of Jesus, Son of the eternal Father,
Heart of Jesus, formed by the Holy Ghost, in the womb
 of the Virgin Mother,
Heart of Jesus, substantially united to the Word of God,
Heart of Jesus, of infinite majesty.
Heart of Jesus, sacred temple of God,
Heart of Jesus, tabernacle of the Most High,
Heart of Jesus, house of God and gate of heaven,
Heart of Jesus, burning furnace of charity,
Heart of Jesus, abode of justice and love,
Heart of Jesus, full of goodness and love,
Heart of Jesus, abyss of all virtues, Heart of Jesus, most
 worthy of all praise,
Heart of Jesus, king and center of all hearts,
Heart of Jesus, in Whom are all the treasures of wisdom
 and knowledge, Heart of Jesus, in Whom dwells the

fulness of divinity,
Heart of Jesus, in Whom the Father was well pleased,
Heart of Jesus, of Whose fullness we have all received,
Heart of Jesus, desire of the everlasting hills,
Heart of Jesus, patient and most merciful,
Heart of Jesus, enriching all who invoke Thee,
Heart of Jesus, fountain of life and holiness,
Heart of Jesus, propitiation for our sins,
Heart of Jesus, loaded down with opprobrium,
Heart of Jesus, bruised for our offences,
Heart of Jesus, obedient unto death,
Heart of Jesus, pierced with a lance,
Heart of Jesus, source of all consolation,
Heart of Jesus, our life and resurrection,
Heart of Jesus, our peace and reconciliation,
Heart of Jesus, victim of sinners,
Heart of Jesus, salvation of those who trust in Thee,
Heart of Jesus, hope of those who die in Thee,
Heart of Jesus, delight of all the Saints,
Lamb of God Who takest away the sins of the world,—*Spare us, O Lord.*
Lamb of God Who takest away the sins of the world,—*Graciously hear us, O Lord.*
Lamb of God Who takest away the sins of the world,—*Have mercy on us.*

V. Jesus, meek and humble of heart, R. Make our hearts like unto Thine.

Let us pray:

O Almighty and eternal God, look upon the Heart of Thy dearly beloved Son, and upon the praise and satisfaction He offers Thee in the name of sinners and for those who seek Thy mercy. Be Thou appeased and grant us pardon in the name of the same Jesus Christ, Thy Son, Who liveth and reigneth with Thee, in the unity of the Holy Ghost, world without end. Amen.

(Ind. of 300 days, once a day).

V.
The Immaculate Conception of the Blessed Virgin Mary

Mary in her Immaculate Conception conquered the devil. For God said to the serpent after the fall of man: "I will put enmity between thee and the Woman, between thy seed and her seed; She shall crush thy head, and thou shalt lie in wait for her heel." This singular privilege is most dear to Mary, therefore, when she appeared at Lourdes, and was asked her name, Mary said: "I am the Immaculate Conception." At one of these miraculous apparitions, Mary specially ordered Bernadette to "Pray for the Sinners and to do Penance." The special devotion to the Immaculate Conception will be then a great help to the members to obtain through Mary Immaculate powerful graces for the poorest of sinners, the Dying Sinners. May then the Immaculate Conception again conquer the devil in the souls of the Dying, and thus prove to be the best Mother for the Poor Dying Sinners.

If you are a child of St. Francis, know that the devotion to the Immaculate Conception is the great inheritance and special glory of the Seraphic Order through the great Defender of Mary Immaculate, the blessed John

Duns Scotus. For the love of Mary foster a great veneration to this great servant of God, since Mary entrusted to him the defense of her dearest privilege. Love to say the Rosary and the special prayers in honor of Mary Immaculate and offer them up for the Dying Sinners.

The Franciscan Rosary and the Seven Joys of Mary Immaculate

This Rosary consists of seven Decades and each decade of one Our Father, ten Hail Mary's and one Glory be to the Father.

For the seven joyful mysteries add after the word of Jesus in the Hail Mary:

1) Whom thou, Immaculate Virgin Mary with joy didst conceive by the Holy Ghost.

2) Whom thou, Immaculate Virgin Mary with joy didst carry to Elizabeth.

3) Whom thou, Immaculate Virgin Mary with joy didst bear in Bethlehem.

4) Whom thou, Immaculate Virgin Mary with joy didst offer to the Magi for adoration.

5) Whom thou, Immaculate Virgin Mary with joy didst find again in the temple.

6) Whom thou, Immaculate Virgin Mary with joy didst

first see again after His Resurrection.
7) Who assumed and crowned thee Immaculate Virgin Mary with joy the Queen of Heaven.

Add two *Hail Mary's* in honor of the 72 years of Mary and one *Our Father, Hail Mary*, and *Glory be to the Father*, ... for the intention of the Holy Father to gain the Plenary Indulgence granted to all the members, of the 3 Orders of St. Francis, whenever they say this Rosary (Sept. 7, 1901).

Saturday, Specially Devoted to Mary Immaculate
A beautiful devotion for Saturday in honor of Mary Immaculate is:

The Little Rosary of the Immaculate Conception

In the name of the Father, and the Son, and the Holy Ghost. Amen.
1) I give Thee thanks, eternal Heavenly Father, because by Thy Omnipotence Thou hast preserved the Blessed Virgin Mary, Thy Daughter, from all stain of original sin. Then say one *Our Father*, 4 *Hail Mary's*, and after each these words:
"Blessed be the holy, most pure, and Immaculate Conception of the Blessed Virgin Mary." Then *Glory be*

to the Father, ...

2) I give Thee thanks, eternal Divine Son, because by Thy Wisdom Thou hast preserved the Blessed Virgin Mary, Thy Mother, from all stain of original sin. *Our Father ...* 4 *Hail Mary's*, and after each *Hail Mary* these words:
"Blessed be the holy, most pure, and Immaculate Conception of the Blessed Virgin Mary." *Then Glory be to the Father, ...*

3) I give Thee thanks, eternal Holy- Ghost, because by Thy Love Thou hast preserved the Blessed Virgin Mary, Thy Spouse, from all stain of original sin. *Our Father ...* 4 *Hail Mary's*, and after each *Hail Mary* these words:
"Blessed be the holy, most pure, and Immaculate Conception of the Blessed Virgin Mary."
Then *Glory be to the Father, ...*

The Three Hail Mary's in Honor of Mary Immaculate

Accustom yourself to say them frequently, if possible, every morning and evening. Add to each Hail Mary the following invocations:

"O Mary, conceived without stain of original sin, Pray

for us, who have recourse to thee."
(100 days, once a day, March 15, 1884).

"Sweet Heart of Mary, be my Salvation."
(300 days each time, Sept. 30, 1852)

The Memorare

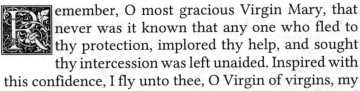emember, O most gracious Virgin Mary, that never was it known that any one who fled to thy protection, implored thy help, and sought thy intercession was left unaided. Inspired with this confidence, I fly unto thee, O Virgin of virgins, my Mother! To thee I come; before thee I stand, sinful and sorrowful. O Mother of the Word Incarnate! despise not my petitions, but in thy mercy hear and answer me. Amen.
(300 days, Dec. 11, 1846)

"O Mary, who didst come into this world free from stain obtain of God for me that I may leave it without sin."
(100 days, March 27, 1863).

Litany of the Blessed Virgin Mary

Kyrie, eleison
Christe, eleison.
Kyrie, eleison.
Christe, audi nos.
Christe, exaudi nos.
Pater de caelis, Deus,
 miserere nobis.
Fili, Redemptor mundi,
 Deus, *miserere nobis.*
Spiritus Sancte Deus,
 miserere nobis.
Sancta Trinitas, unus Deus,
 miserere nobis.
Sancta Maria, *ora pro nobis.*
Sancta Dei Genetrix,
Sancta Virgo virginum,
Mater Christi,
Mater Ecclesiae,
Mater Divinae gratiae,
Mater purissima,
Mater castissima,
Mater inviolata,
Mater intemerata,
Mater amabilis,
Mater admirabilis,
Mater boni Consilii,
Mater Creatoris,
Mater Salvatoris,

Lord, have mercy on us,
 Christ have mercy on us.
Lord, have mercy on us.
 Christ, hear us.
Christ graciously hear us.
God, the Father of heaven,
 have mercy on us.
God the Son, Redeemer of
 the world, *have mercy on us.*
God the Holy Ghost,
 have mercy on us.
Holy Trinity, one God,
 have mercy on us.
Holy Mary, *pray for us.*
Holy Mother of God,
Holy Virgin of virgins,
Mother of Christ,
Mother of the Church
Mother of divine grace,
Mother most pure,
Mother most chaste,
Mother inviolate,
Mother undefiled,
Mother most amiable,
Mother most admirable,
Mother of good counsel,
Mother of our Creator,
Mother of our Savior,

Virgo prudentissima,	Virgin most prudent,
Virgo veneranda,	Virgin most venerable,
Virgo praedicanda,	Virgin most renowned,
Virgo potens,	Virgin most powerful,
Virgo clemens,	Virgin most merciful,
Virgo fidelis,	Virgin most faithful,
Speculum iustitiae,	Mirror of justice,
Sedes sapientiae,	Seat of wisdom,
Causa nostrae laetitiae,	Cause of our joy,
Vas spirituale,	Spiritual vessel,
Vas honorabile,	Vessel of honor,
Vas insigne devotionis,	Singular vessel of devotion,
Rosa mystica,	Mystical rose,
Turris Davidica,	Tower of David,
Turris eburnea,	Tower of ivory,
Domus aurea,	House of gold,
Foederis arca,	Ark of the covenant,
Ianua caeli,	Gate of heaven,
Stella matutina,	Morning star,
Salus infirmorum,	Health of the sick,
Refugium peccatorum,	Refuge of sinners,
Consolatrix afflictorum,	Comforter of the afflicted,
Auxilium Christianorum,	Help of Christians,
Regina Angelorum,	Queen of Angels,
Regina Patriarcharum,	Queen of Patriarchs,
Regina Prophetarum,	Queen of Prophets,
Regina Apostolorum,	Queen of Apostles,
Regina Martyrum,	Queen of Martyrs,
Regina Confessorum,	Queen of Confessors,

Regina Virginum,
Regina Sanctorum omnium,
Regina sine labe originali
 concepta,
Regina in caelum assumpta,
Regina Sanctissimi Rosarii,

Regina familiae,
Regina pacis,

Agnus Dei, qui tollis peccata
 mundi,
parce nobis, Domine.
Agnus Dei, qui tollis peccata
 mundi,
exaudi nobis, Domine.
Agnus Dei, qui tollis peccata
 mundi,
miserere nobis.
Ora pro nobis, Sancta Dei
Genetrix,
Ut digni efficiamur
promissionibus Christi.

Oremus.

Concede nos famulos tuos,
quaesumus, Domine Deus,
perpetua mentis et corporis
sanitate gaudere: et gloriosa

Queen of Virgins,
Queen of all Saints,
Queen conceived without
 original sin,
Queen assumed into heaven,
Queen of the most holy
 Rosary.

Queen of the family,
Queen of Peace,

Lamb of God, who takest
 away the sins of the world,
 spare us, O Lord.
Lamb of God, who takest
 away the sins of the world,
 graciously hear us O Lord.
Lamb of God, who takest
 away the sins of the world,
 have mercy on us.
Pray for us, O holy Mother
of God. (That we may be
made worthy of the
promises of Christ.)

Let us pray.

Grant, we beseech Thee, O
Lord God, unto us Thy
servants, that we may rejoice
in continual health of mind

beatae Mariae semper Virginis intercessione, a praesenti liberari tristitia, et aeterna perfrui laetitia. Per Christum Dominum nostrum. *Amen.*

and body; and, by the glorious intercession of Blessed Mary ever Virgin, may be delivered from present sadness, and enter into the joy of Thine eternal gladness. Through Christ our Lord. *Amen.*

Prayer in Honor of Mary's Holy Death for a Happy Death

Mary, our Immaculate Mother, how holy and how happy was thy death caused by thy most ardent love and desired for Thy Divine Son. Great will be our need of help when our last hour will come! Dear Mother, for this hour of our death, we now ask thy most special intercession with the good and merciful Lord that in view of thy most happy death and for the love with which thou after the example of thy dearest Son didst freely choose death, He may help us by placing us. like St. John, under thy special maternal protection. Shield us then against the wicked enemy, and assist us at the last moment that we may die free from mortal sin and confirmed in the grace and love of God. After our death lead us to the throne of Mercy and there obtain for us and all the Poor Dying Sinners from thy Divine Son a merciful judgment. Amen

Devotion to the Sorrowful Mother of God

Mary Immaculate suffered with her Divine Son and offered up all her sufferings in union with the bitter Passion and Death of Jesus Christ for the Salvation of the poor sinners. It will therefore please Mary Immaculate, if we piously venerate her sorrows and ask her compassionate motherly heart to offer them up again for the Poor Dying Sinners. The following prayers may be used for this purpose:

Prayer to the Compassionate Heart of Mary

O sweetest mother Mary, refuge of sinners and comforter of the afflicted, we pray thee, by the sorrows of thy immaculate Heart and by the agony of the Heart of Jesus, thy most be loved Son, intercede for all sinners that are now in their agony. Show thyself a kind mother to all souls oppressed with sorrow and afflictions. Amen.

Compassionate Heart of Mary, pray for the dying and afflicted.

Prayer to Mary at the Foot of the Cross

Mary, glorious and blessed Virgin, A who didst die consumed by the fire of divine love, pray for us, poor sinners, now and at the hour of our death. Do not forsake us unfortunate children at the last moment. Thou, who wast standing at the foot of the cross of thy dying Son, accept now the last sighs of those that invoke thee with full confidence. Remember that death, which was a triumph for thee, is a chastisement for us. Have pity on so many unfortunate children who call thee their mother and their hope. Pray for us all, assist us all. Obtain for us the grace to bear our sufferings with patience, and generously to make to God the sacrifice of our life. Amen.

Prayer to Our Lady of Sorrows

O, most merciful Virgin Mary, help of Christians, and consolation of afflicted souls, I entreat thee, through thy most compassionate heart, and by the agony of Jesus thy beloved Son, to obtain for me and for all those whom it shall please our Lord to try by affliction, sufferings, or temptation, especially at the last hour, the grace to bear them with perfect resignation, to accept them with cordial submission, to unite them to the holy dispositions of thy most afflicted heart, and of the Agonizing Heart of thy Divine Son. Sanctify them, that they may be meritorious for me, serve as an expiation for my faults, and help to save sinners, particularly those who are in their agony.

Obtain for us, O Queen of Martyrs, at each new trial, the strength and courage to say with the great Model of the afflicted: "My Father, if this chalice cannot pass unless I drink it, not my will, but Thine, be done." Amen.

VI.
Devotion to St. Michael, the Holy Angels, and Our Patron Saints

St. Michael led the battle of God in heaven against the bad angels. He will therefore gladly assist us with his good angels, especially the Guardian Angels, to obtain another victory over satan by the Salvation of the Dying Sinners. Also our good Patron-Saints will help us by their intercession at the throne of mercy and thus become our power- full allies in the good cause.

Recommendation of St. Michael, Protector of Souls

glorious Archangel, St. Michael, who didst fight with so great courage against the rebellious angels, come to the assistance of the Dying. Behold with what fury the demons surround them! See with what perfidy Satan strives to keep them in the chains of sin, to make their hearts obdurate, and finally to cast them into hell! O loving protector of souls, hasten to assist the Dying. Excite in them the sentiments of a lively faith and sincere contrition, reanimate their confidence, enkindle in their hearts the fire of divine love, alleviate their sufferings, obtain for them the grace of resignation, defend them in their agony, and after having assisted them to gain the victory, conduct them to the abode of the elect. Amen.

Prayer to the Guardian Angels of the Dying.

Blessed Guardian Angels, I pray you by the Agonizing Heart of Jesus and the Compassionate Heart of Mary, your Immaculate Queen, intercede the Dying entrusted to your care. Preserve them from evil, confirm them in all virtue, deliver them from the snares of Satan, that by your assistance they may obtain the grace of a happy death and after death be admitted to the company of the Saints. Amen.

Prayer to the Angel that Comforted Jesus Agonizing in the Garden of Olives

holy Angel who didst comfort Jesus agonizing in the garden of Olives, deign to strengthen those who are now struggling with death. Intercede for them! Secure to them strength and courage to resist the assaults of the demon, to bear their sufferings with patience, and to make willingly to God the sacrifice of their life. Ask their Guardian Angels their Patron Saints, and the whole celestial court to obtain for them all the graces and to come to their assistance.... Ask above all the Queen of Angels, the August Mother of God, to protect the Dying by her powerful assistance and to be their advocate with her Divine Son Jesus that He may show mercy and give them the grace of a happy death. Amen.

Prayer to Our Holy rather St. Francis.

O holy Father, St. Francis, thou perfect image of our Crucified Savior, who by thy meditation on the sufferings of Jesus, thy singular devotion to the Blessed Sacrament, and thy love for Mary, the Queen of Angels, didst fill thy Seraphic heart not only with most ardent love for God, but also with the greatest desire to convert and save the poor sinners, help us by thy powerful intercession to imitate thy holy example, often to meditate on the bitter Passion of Christ, to foster a special love for Jesus in the Blessed Sacrament, and His dear mother, Mary Immaculate, and to save many a Poor Dying Sinner for all eternity. Amen.

Prayer of the Church to St. Camillus, Patron of the Dying

O God, Who for the protection of souls struggling in their last agony hast adorned St. Camillus with a singular prerogative of charity, grant us by his merits the spirit of Thy charity that we may merit to conquer the enemy in the hour of death and to attain to the heavenly crown, through Jesus Christ, our Lord. Amen.

Prayer to St. Barbara.

Grant, O Lord, through the intercession of St. Barbara, that before our death we may worthily receive the holy Sacraments of Penance. Eucharist, and Extreme Unction, through Christ, our Lord. Amen.

Invocation of the Patron Saints of the Confraternity.

Agonizing Heart of Jesus, have mercy on the Dying.
Compassionate Heart of Mary, pray for the Dying.
St. Joseph, Patron of a happy death, pray for the Dying.
St. Michael, the Archangel, protector of souls, pray for the Dying.
Holy Guardian Angels, and Patron Saints of the Dying, pray for the Dying.
St. John and St. Magdalene, who assisted at the Agony and Death of Jesus on the cross, pray for the Dying.
Seraphic St. Francis, perfect image of our crucified Savior, pray for the Dying.
St. Camillus of Lellis, and St. John of God, favored with the gifts of assisting souls in the last struggle of death, pray for the Dying.
St. Barbara, who dost obtain for thy clients the grace worthily to receive the last Sacraments before death, pray for the Dying.
Holy Penitent Thief, who at the last moment didst hear from the mouth of Jesus the consoling words: "This day thou shalt be with me in paradise," pray for the Dying Sinners.

VII.
The Best Manner of Practically Helping Dying Persons.

There is no greater consolation than to be instrumental, in saving immortal souls for heaven. Any one may be called upon to perform this act of charity and should therefore well know what he should do for a dying person in case of necessity. The Dying may be either unbaptized children, or grown-up Catholics, Protestants, or Infidels.

I.
How to Help Dying Children.

If you see a child dying that is not yet baptized, and you well know that the parents in no way object to the baptism of the child, baptize in the following manner:

Private Baptism of Dying Children
Take any kind of natural water, pour the water over the forehead of the child, and, while pouring the water, say carefully these words: "I baptize thee in the name of the Father, and of the Son, and of the Holy Ghost." Should the child die, you have the consolation of having made it a child of God and of heaven forever. If you know or

fear that the parents would not consent to the baptism of the child, and the child is surely dying, you may take a wet towel or wet sponge and wipe off the forehead of the child in such a manner that a few drops of water will flow from the forehead of the child, and while wiping the forehead, say, without being heard by the other, the words: "I baptize thee in the name of the Father, and of the Son, and of the Holy Ghost."

Physicians, Nurses, Midwives, and Mothers should never forget that life is present from the moment of conception, and therefore any human form brought forth, no matter at what stage of development, should be baptized in the best way possible. What a terrible crime to destroy the early life and deprive the poor child of the possibility of being baptized!

Catholic parents should be warned never to postpone or neglect the baptism of their new-born children that these little children may not die without holy baptism. Catholic children that have arrived at the use of reason and are dangerously sick, should be prepared for death by the holy sacraments of Penance, Eucharist, and Extreme Unction.

II. How to Help Dying Catholic Adults

If a grown-up Catholic is very sick and in danger of

death, call the priest and inform him of it even if the patient or his family does not want it. It may be only foolish fear on the part of the patient or the members of the family. Try to prepare in the sick room every thing necessary for the proper administration of the holy Sacraments. Upon a little table covered with white cloth, place a crucifix between two blessed candles which are lighted while the holy Sacraments are administered. Have at hand a small white cloth to be used by the patient for holy Communion, a glass of fresh water, a clean spoon, and on a plate some clean cotton.

After the sick person has been prepared for death by the priest, the patient may live yet for some hours or days. If the death struggle sets in, and the priest is not at hand, light the blessed candles, put into the hand of the dying person or hold for him the crucifix that he may kiss it, sprinkle him with holy water, and then make with him or for him acts of faith, hope, charity, contrition, and resignation to God's holy will, as the following:

Acts or Short Prayers to Be Made With or For Dying Persons

O my God, I believe in Thee, eternal Truth.

O my God, I hope in Thee, eternal Goodness.

O my God, I love Thee above all things, my highest and supreme Good, and I love my neighbor as myself for the love of Thee.

O my God, I forgive all who have injured or offended me and I ask pardon of all whom I have injured or offended.

O my God, I hate and detest all my sins and I am heartily sorry for them because by them I have offended Thee Thou Infinite Good. With the help of Thy grace I will never offend Thee again. O Jesus forgive me all my sins and grant me the grace of a happy death.

O my God, I accept death with full resignation to Thy holy will as atonement for all my sins and in union with the most bitter death of Jesus Christ.

My Jesus, Mercy!

Sweet Heart of Jesus, be my love!

Sweetest Jesus, be not my judge, but a Savior!

Sweet Heart of Mary, be my Salvation!

Dearest Mother Mary, Immaculate Virgin, do not forsake me now, but save thy child!

St. Joseph, Patron of a happy death, come with Jesus and Mary to help me.

Holy Guardian Angel, protect me against the evil spirits.

Holy Patron Saint, pray for me.

St. Michael, and all ye holy Angels and Saints of God, assist me in my last struggle and pray for me and all the

Poor Dying Sinners. Amen.

If no priest is present, sprinkle the dying person repeatedly with holy water, and then kneeling at the bed pray with those present the Litany of the Dying and the Recommendation of a departing soul as on (pages 141 and 143.)

III.
How to Help Dying Non-Catholics

If the dying person is an infidel that was never baptized, ask him whether he would not like to die a Christian and be baptized before his death, and, of he consents to it, and no priest can be called, or, if you fear the priest may come too late, make with the dying person the acts of faith, hope, charity, and contrition and then baptize him the same way as little children are baptized, in case of necessity (p. 132.)

If the dying person is a baptized Protestant who believes his religion to be the right one and expresses no desire of becoming a Catholic, tell him that you wish to pray for him such prayers as every good Christian should say before he dies. Then make with him short acts of faith, hope, and charity, but above all an act of perfect contrition, as it may be the only means of saving that dying person.

Dear members of the "Pious Union for the Salvation of the Dying," read carefully the following remarks about Perfect Contrition.

IV. Perfect Contrition, the Great Means of Eternal Salvation.

Know well, my dear friend, and never forget it, that for many dying persons an Act of Perfect Contrition is the only means of their Eternal Salvation. If any person is in the state of mortal sin, an act of Perfect Contrition made before he dies will save his soul. Therefore, every Catholic should well learn how to make an Act of Perfect Contrition so that he can make it easily whenever he needs it himself or when he should make it for a dying person whom he assists in the last hour. What is Contrition? Contrition is a real hatred and detestation of all our sins and a hearty sorrow for them, that means, an ardent wish not to have committed them, because by them we have offended God, the highest Good. To this hatred and sorrow for our sins must necessarily be joined the firm will not to offend God any more by sin, but to love and serve Him faithfully. Now, always keep in mind: Without GOOD

Contrition there is no forgiveness of our sins. But when will our Contrition obtain from God pardon of our sins? First, when it comes really from our heart and will; secondly, when it extends at least to all our mortal sins; thirdly when it is truly supernatural. Some people are really sorry for their sins, because by them they offended some other person, or brought disgrace and temporal loss and punishment upon themselves. This is a merely natural contrition which can not obtain pardon from God, as it does not refer to God. If God is to forgive our sins, our Contrition must also come from God; it must be supernatural. What, then, will make our Contrition supernatural? First, the grace of God. But God will always give us this grace, if we humbly ask for it. Therefore, before making an Act of Contrition ask God for this special grace. Secondly, our Contrition must proceed from a supernatural motive, that is, a motive which we know by the light of our holy faith. Such motives are: "That mortal sin is the greatest evil in the sight of God; that we have been most ungrateful to God, our greatest benefactor; that we have offended the infinite Majesty of God; that we have lost God and heaven and deserve to be punished by God in the eternal flames of hell; that we have caused the sufferings and bitter death of Jesus Christ; that we did not love God, the highest and best Good." Some of these motives are better or more perfect than others and thus our Contrition may be perfect or imperfect. Our Contrition is only imperfect when it proceeds chiefly from the fear of God's punishments, because by mortal sin we have lost God's grace and heaven and deserved hell. This Contrition is sufficient with the Absolution of the priest. But, if we can not receive the Absolution of the priest *only perfect Contrition* can obtain pardon of our mortal sins. When is our Contrition perfect? Our Contrition is perfect, when it proceeds from the pure and perfect love of God, that means, when we hate our sins and are sorry for them chiefly for God's sake, because we did not love Him, the highest and most amiable Good Whom we should have loved above all things. This perfect Contrition must also include the firm will never more to offend God by mortal sin, but to love Him sincerely and to obey all His commandments. Such perfect Contrition will immediately remit the guilt of mortal sin, even outside of Confession. However, the mortal sin thus forgiven must yet be confessed in the next Confession. Make this act of Perfect Contrition, whenever you had the misfortune of committing a mortal sin and cannot go to Confession at once. Make is before receiving the holy Sacraments, as it will purify your soul the more. Make it before you go to bed and in every danger of death, as it may be your only means of eternal Salvation. Help also others to make it, especially whenever you assist a Dying Person. Before you make it, first pray for God's grace, then look piously at the crucifix, consider how much Jesus, your loving Redeemer, suffered all this and even died for your sins. This love of Jesus crucified will best move you to perfect Contrition, for which you may use the following prayer:

An Act of Perfect Contrition

O my God, with the help of Thy grace for which I now humbly ask Thee, I hate and detest all my sins, and I am heartily sorry for them, because by these sins I have offended Thee and did not love Thee, the Infinite Good, my best Father and most loving Redeemer, Who even suffered and died for my sins on the Cross. I humbly ask pardon of all my sins and I firmly hope to receive forgiveness through the Precious Blood of Jesus Christ, my dearest Savior. I am fully resolved and faithfully promise with the help of Thy grace never more to offend Thee, but to love Thee above all things, and my neighbor as myself for the love of Thee. My Jesus, mercy. Amen.

VIII.
The Prayers of the Church for the Dying.

Litany for the Dying.

Lord, *have mercy on him (or her).*
Christ, *have mercy on him.*
Lord, *have mercy on him.*
Holy Mary, *pray for him (or her).*
All ye holy Angels and Archangels, *pray for him (or her).*
Holy Abel,
All ye choirs of the Just,
Holy Abraham,
St. John Baptist,
St. Joseph,
All ye holy Patriarchs and Prophets,
St. Peter,
St. Paul,
St. Andrew,
St. John,
All ye holy Apostles and Evangelists,
All ye holy disciples of our Lord,
St. Stephen,
St. Lawrence,
All ye holy Martyrs,

St. Sylvester,
St. Gregory,
St. Augustine,
All ye holy Bishops and Confessors,
St. Benedict,
St. Francis,
St. Camillus of Lellis and St. John of God,
All ye holy Monks and Hermits,
St. Mary Magdalene,
St. Lucy,
All ye holy Virgins and Widows, *intercede for him (or her).*
Be merciful unto him, O God, *Spare him (or her), O Lord.*
Be merciful unto him. *Deliver him (or her), O Lord.*
From Thy wrath, *deliver him (or her), O Lord.*
From the danger of eternal death,
From an evil death,
From the pains of hell,
From all evil,
From the power of the devil,
By Thy Nativity,
By Thy Cross and Passion,
By Thy Death and Burial,
By Thy glorious Resurrection,
By Thy wonderful Ascension,
By the grace of the Holy Ghost, the Comforter,

In the day of Judgment,
We sinners beseech Thee to hear us.
That Thou spare him, we beseech Thee to hear us.
Lord, *have mercy on him.*
Christ, *have mercy on him.*
Lord, *have mercy on him.*

Recommendation of a Departing Soul

o forth, O Christian soul, out of this world, in the name of God, the Father Almighty, Who created thee; in the name of Jesus Christ, the Son of the living God, Who suffered for thee; in the name of the Holy Ghost, Who sanctified thee; in the name of the glorious and holy Virgin Mary, Mother of God; in the name of blessed Joseph, the glorious Spouse of the same Virgin; in the name of the Angels, Archangels, Thrones, and Dominations, Cherubim and Seraphim; in the name of the Patriarchs and Prophets, of the holy Apostles and Evangelists, of the Holy Martyrs, Confessors, Monks and Hermits, of the holy Virgins, and of all the Saints of God. May thy place be this day in peace, and thy abode in holy Sion. Through Christ, our Lord. Amen.

O merciful and gracious God! O God, Who according to the multitude of Thy mercies blottest out the sins of such as repent, and graciously remittest the guilt of their past offences, mercifully regard this Thy servant, N., and grant him (or her) full remission of all his sins, who with a contrite heart most earnestly begs it of Thee. Renew, O merciful Father, whatever has been vitiated in him, by human frailty or by the frauds and deceits of the enemy; and associate him as a member of redemption to the unity of the body of the Church. Have compassion, O Lord, on his sighs, have compassion on his tears, and admit him who has no hope but in Thy mercy, to the sacrament of Thy reconciliation. Through Christ, our Lord. Amen.

I commend thee, dear brother, to the Almighty God, and consign thee to the care of Him, whose creature thou art, that, when thou shalt have paid the debt of all mankind by death, thou mayest return to Thy Maker, Who formed thee from the dust of the earth. When, therefore, thy soul shall depart from thy body, may the resplendent multitude of the Angels meet thee; may the court of the Apostles receive thee; may the triumphant army of glorious Martyrs come out to welcome thee; may the splendid company of Confessors, clad in their white robes, encompass thee; may the choir of joyful Virgins receive thee; and mayest thou meet with the blessed repose in the bosom of the Patriarchs. May St. Joseph, the most sweet patron of the Dying, raise thee to a great height. May the holy Virgin Mary, Mother of God kindly turn her eyes to thee. May Jesus Christ appear to thee with a mild and joyful countenance, and appoint thee a place amongst those who are to stand before Him forever. Mayest thou be a stranger to all that is punished with darkness, chastised with flames, and condemned to torments. May the most wicked enemy, with all his evil spirits, be forced to give way; may he tremble at thy approach in the company of Angels, and with confusion fly away into the vast chaos of eternal night. Let God arise and His enemies be dispersed, and let them that hate Him fly before His face, let them vanish like smoke; and as wax that melts before the fire, so let sinners perish in the sight of God; but may the just rejoice and be happy in His presence. May then all the legions of hell be confounded and put to shame; and may none of the ministers of Satan dare stop thee on thy way. May Christ deliver thee from torments, Who was crucified for thee. May He deliver thee in the ever-verdant lawns of His safety to die for thee. May Jesus Christ, the Son of the living God, place thee from eternal death, Who vouch Paradise, and may He, the true Shepherd, acknowledge thee as one of His flock. May He absolve thee from all thy sins, and place thee at His right hand in the midst of His Elect. Mayest thou see thy Redeemer face to face, and, standing, always in His presence, behold with happy eyes the most clear truth. And mayest thou be placed among the companies of the Blessed, and enjoy the sweetness of the contemplation of thy God forever. Amen.

Prayer to the Blessed Virgin Mary for a Dying Person

most clement Virgin Mary, Mother of God, the most pious consoler of the afflicted, do thou commend the soul of this servant N., to Thy Son that by thy maternal intercession he (she) may not fear the terrors of death, but in thy company reach joyfully the longed for mansion of the heavenly home. Amen.

Prayer to St. Joseph for a Dying Person

St. Joseph, Patron of the Dying, to thee I have recourse and, since at thy departure from this world Jesus and Mary assisted thee with loving care, I now through this twofold dearest pledge earnestly recommend to thee the soul of this servant N., who is now struggling in his (her) last agony, that by thy protection he (she) may be delivered from the snares of the devil and from eternal death and merit to reach the eternal joys. Through the same Christ, our Lord. Amen.

At the moment of death invoke the sweet name "Jesus" and say with Christ: "Father, into Thy hands I commend my spirit." Jesus, Mary, Joseph, may I breathe forth my soul in peace with you. When the person is dead, kneel down to say a few prayers for the repose of the departed soul.

IX.
Litany for a Happy Death
To Our Lord Jesus Christ

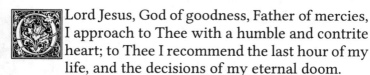Lord Jesus, God of goodness, Father of mercies, I approach to Thee with a humble and contrite heart; to Thee I recommend the last hour of my life, and the decisions of my eternal doom.

When my feet, benumbed with death, shall admonish me that my mortal course is drawing to an end, Merciful Jesus, have mercy on me.

When my eyes, dim and troubled at the approach of death, shall fix themselves on Thee, my last and only support, Merciful Jesus, have mercy on me.

When my face, pale and livid, shall inspire the beholders with pity and dismay, Merciful Jesus, have mercy on me. When my head shall forebode my approaching end,

Merciful Jesus, have mercy on me.

When my ears, soon forever to be shut to the discourse of men, shall be open to the irrevocable decree which is to cut me off from the number of the living, Merciful Jesus, have mercy on me.

When my imagination, agitated by dreadful spectres, shall be sunk in an abyss of anguish, Merciful Jesus, have mercy on me.

When my soul, affrighted with the sight of my iniquities, and the terrors of Thy judgment, shall have to fight against the angel of darkness, who will endeavor to conceal Thy mercies from my eyes, and to plunge me into despair, Merciful Jesus, have mercy on me.

When my poor heart, yielding to the pressure and exhausted by its frequent struggles against the enemies of its salvation, shall feel the pangs of death, Merciful Jesus, have mercy on me.

When the last tear, the forerunner of my dissolution, shall drop from my eyes, receive it as a sacrifice of expiation for my sins. Grant that I may expire the victim of penance, and in that dreadful moment, Merciful Jesus, have mercy on me.

When my friends and relations encircling my bed, shall shed tears of pity over me, and invoke Thy clemency in my behalf, Merciful Jesus, have mercy on me.

When I have lost the use of my senses, when the world shall have vanished from my sight, when my agonizing soul shall feel the sorrow of death, Merciful Jesus, have mercy on me.

When my last sigh shall summon my soul to burst from the embraces of the body, and to spring to Thee on the wings of impatience and desire, Merciful Jesus, have mercy on me.

When my soul, trembling on my lips, shall bid adieu to the world, and leave my body lifeless, pale, and cold, receive the separation as a homage, which I willingly pay to Thy Divine Majesty. In that last moment of my mortal life, Merciful Jesus, have mercy on me.

When at length, my soul admitted to Thy presence, shall first behold the splendors of Thy Majesty reject me not, but receive me into Thy bosom, where I may forever sing Thy praises, In that moment when eternity shall begin to me, Merciful Jesus, have mercy on me. Amen.

TO THE ETERNAL FATHER

O God, Who hast condemned us to die, but concealed the hour and moment of death from us, grant that I may spend all the days of my life in justice and holiness and thereby merit to depart from this world in Thy holy love through the merits of our Lord Jesus Christ, Who

with Thee liveth and reigneth in unity of the Holy
Ghost. Amen.
(100 days, once a day.)

"God is charity, and he that abideth in charity abideth in
God and God in him" says St. John in his epistle. And
again: "In this we have known the charity of God
because he hath laid down his life for us and we ought
to lay down our lives for the brethren."

X.
Stations of the Cross for the Dying

Preparatory Prayer

N. B. First reflect a little on the mystery represented by the station, then applying it to the Dying, say the prayer at each station, after which add the following ejaculations for the Dying and, as it were, in their stead:

"My Jesus mercy."
(300 days.)

"Sweetest Jesus, be not to me a Judge, but a Savior."
(50 days.)

"Sweet Heart of Mary, be my salvation."
(300 days.)

"Jesus, Mary, Joseph, assist me in my last agony."
(100 days.)

Or "O most Merciful Jesus, lover of souls." . . . the daily prayer for the Dying, (page 74).

Preparatory Prayer

O Agonizing Heart of Jesus! to assist the Dying in their greatest struggle, I now desire to follow Thee with Mary, Thy compassionate Mother, on the holy way of the Cross. Cleanse my heart from all sins, and uniting my prayers with the merits of Thy bitter Passion and Death, do Thou offer them to Thy Heavenly Father, to obtain a happy death for all the agonizing. I also intend to gain all the Indulgences, granted to this devotion, for the poor souls in purgatory. Have mercy, O sweetest Jesus, on all our suffering brethren, both the Dying and the dead. Amen.

✠

I. Station.
(Jesus is condemned to death.)

O Jesus, Who wast innocently condemned to death, be now a merciful Judge to the Dying. Grant them the efficacious grace of conversion, that Thou mayest not condemn them to the eternal death of hell Amen. ("My Jesus mercy," "Sweetest Jesus, etc." . . . as above.)

✠

II. Station.
(Jesus taking the Cross.)

O Jesus Who didst willingly take up Thy Cross for our salvation, bestow now upon all Dying Sinners the grace to bear their sufferings with patience, and to accept death with resignation as an atonement for their many sins. Amen. (My Jesus, mercy." . . .

✠

III. Station.
(Jesus falling the first time.)

O Jesus, by the sufferings Thou didst endure, and by the Blood Thou didst shed in Thy first fall under the Cross, deign to raise the Dying from their fall into sin and vice, and graciously preserve them from being plunged into the abyss of hell. Amen.

✠

IV. Station.
(Jesus met by Mary.)

O Jesus and Mary, by the pain you felt at seeing each other so much afflicted, hasten to the assistance of the

Dying, that so many and so great sufferings may not be rendered fruitless in their souls by the assaults of Satan. Amen.

✠

V. Station.
(Jesus assisted by Simon of Cyrene.)

O Jesus, as Simon assisted Thee in carrying the Cross, do Thou, by offering all Thy sufferings to Thy Heavenly Father, effectually help the Dying to free themselves from the heavy weight of their sins. Amen.

✠

VI. Station.
(Veronica wiping the face of Jesus.)

O Jesus, by the love Thou didst show to Veronica for her kindness, favorably accept our prayers and offerings in behalf of the Dying, and show them now Thy holy Face, by imprinting on their souls Thy holy image, the gift, of sanctifying grace. Amen.

✠

VII. Station.
(Jesus falling the second time.)

O Jesus, by Thy increased sufferings and by the holy Blood shed in Thy second fall, I pray Thee to forgive the Dying their repeated relapses into sin, that their faithlessness and ingratitude may not impede the grace of true conversion. Amen.

✠

VIII. Station
(Jesus consoling the pious women.)

O Jesus, as Thou didst console the pious women who accompanied Thee to Mount Calvary, grant us, who follow Thee on the Way of the Cross, that the Dying may sincerely weep over their sins, to be also comforted by Thee. Amen.

✠

IX. Station.
(Jesus falling the third time.)

O Jesus, by Thy unspeakable pain, and by Thy Precious Blood that flowed to the ground in Thy third fall, remove from the souls of the Dying all obstacles to their conversion, and give them the grace not to yield in their last struggle to their vicious habits and predominant passions. Amen.

✠

X. Station.
(Jesus stripped of His garments.)

O Jesus, by the terrible sufferings Thou didst endure when being stripped of Thy garments, forgive the Dying all their sins of impurity, and let them expire clothed with the garment of sanctifying grace. Amen.

✠

XI. Station.
(Jesus nailed to the Cross.)

O Jesus, by the inexpressible torture Thou didst suffer when being nailed to the Cross, and by Thy Precious Blood which flowed from the wounds of Thy hands and feet, deliver the Dying from the chains of their sins, and from the captivity of Satan and hell. Amen.

✠

XII. Station.
(Jesus dying on the Cross.)

O Jesus, by the infinite merits of Thy Agony and Death on the Cross, assist the Dying in their agony that they may expire in Thy holy grace, and that Thou mayest not have suffered and died in vain for them. Amen.

✠

XIII. Station.
(Jesus placed in the arms of Mary.)

O dolorous Mother of God, so much afflicted at the loss of thy dearest Son, obtain now by the intercession and assistance for all the Dying, the grace not to lose their Savior for all eternity, but to depart in thy arms and united with Jesus in holy love. Amen.

✠

XIV. Station.
(Jesus laid into the Sepulcher.)

O Jesus, as Thou didst rest from Thy sufferings and after three days gloriously rise from the grave, grant that the Dying may be delivered from their pains and, triumphing over sin, satan, and hell, rise to the eternal life of heaven. Amen.

Prayer after the Stations

O Agonizing Heart of Jesus! I thank Thee for all the graces bestowed upon the Dying and upon me during this devotion. In atonement for my many defects do Thou now offer to the Divine Majesty all the holy Masses in which the fruits of Thy bitter Passion and Death are continually renewed, that the Dying may not be lost, and the poor souls be now admitted to the eternal joys of heaven. Amen.

Three *Our Fathers* and *Hail Mary's* in honor of the Agony of Jesus and the Dolors of Mary for the Dying, "O most Merciful Jesus" (pg. 74), etc.

XI.
Acts to be Made for the Moment of Death

The Act of Resignation by which we willingly accept from the hand of God death with all its circumstances is one of the most perfect acts of virtue that we can make. As we may not be able to make it at the moment of death, we should make it during life-time. In order to encourage the faithful to do this, the Church, as a special favor, grants a Plenary Indulgence for the hour of death to all those who make the following Act of Resignation with true love of God after having received the Sacraments of Penance and Holy Eucharist.

I. Act of Resignation.
My Lord and my God! I now already accept death in whatever manner it may come to me according to Thy pleasure. With a resigned and willing heart, I accept death and all its accompanying anxieties, pains, and sufferings as coming from Thy hands.

(Pius X. March 9, 1904.)

II. Act of Offering of One's Death for the Dying

O my God, accepting my death from Thy hands with full

resignation to Thy holy will, I wish to unite it with the Most Bitter Death of Jesus, my Savior, and to offer it up with His great Sacrifice on the Cross in atonement for my many sins, and for the Salvation of those who will die at the same time and appear with me before the Judgment-seat of Thy Son, our Lord and Savior, Jesus Christ, that all may find mercy and salvation. Amen.

O sweetest Jesus, be not to me a Judge, but a Savior. My Jesus, Mercy. Sweet Heart of Mary, be my Salvation. St. Joseph. Patron of a Happy Death, Pray for us and the Poor Dying Sinners. Amen.

APPENDIX

The Most Usual Prayers of a Devout Catholic

The Sign of the Cross:

✠

In the name of the Father, and of the Son, and of the Holy Ghost. Amen.

The Lord's Prayer.

Our Father who art in heaven, hallowed be Thy name, Thy kingdom come, Thy will be done on earth, as it is in heaven. Give us this day our daily bread, and forgive us our trespasses, as we. forgive those that trespass against us. And lead us not into temptation, but deliver us from evil. Amen.

The Angelical Salutation

Hail Mary, full of grace! The Lord is with thee. Blessed art thou amongst women, and blessed is the fruit of thy womb, Jesus. Holy Mary, Mother of God, pray for us sinners, now and at the hour of our death. Amen.

The Apostles' Creed

I believe in God, the Father Almighty, Creator of heaven and earth; and in Jesus Christ, His only Son. our Lord, Who was conceived by the Holy Ghost, born of the Virgin Mary, suffered under Pontius Pilate, was crucified, died, and was buried. He descended into hell, the third day He arose again from the dead; He ascended into heaven, sitteth at the right hand of God, the Father Almighty; from thence He shall come to judge the living and the dead. I believe in the Holy Ghost, the Holy Catholic Church, the communion of Saints, the forgiveness of sins, the resurrection of the body, and life everlasting. Amen.

Confiteor, or General Confession of Sins.

I confess to Almighty God, to Blessed Mary, ever Virgin, to Blessed Michael, the Archangel, to Blessed John the Baptist, to the holy Apostles Peter and Paul, to all the Saints, and to you Father, that I have sinned exceedingly in thought, word and deed, through my fault, through my faut, through my most grievous fault. Therefore, I beseech Blessed Mary, ever Virgin, Blessed Michael, the Archangel, Blessed John the Baptist, the ' holy Apostles Peter and Paul, all the Saints, and you Father, to pray to the Lord, our God for me. Amen.

May the Almighty God have mercy on me, forgive me my sins, and bring me to life everlasting. Amen.

The Angelus
(Three times a day, morning, noon and night.)

V. The angel of the Lord declared unto Mary;

R. And she conceived by the Holy Ghost; Hail Mary, etc.

V. Behold the handmaid of the Lord

R. Be it done to me according to thy word; Hail Mary, etc.

V. And the Word was made flesh;

R. And dwelt among us; Hail Mary, etc.

V. Pray for us, O holy Mother of God;

R. That we may be made worthy of the promises of Christ.

Let us pray:
Pour forth, we beseech Thee, O Lord, Thy grace into our hearts, that we, to whom the Incarnation of Christ, Thy Son, was made known by the message of an angel, may by His passion and cross be brought to the glory of His resurrection, through the same Christ, our Lord. Amen.

The Doxology
(Praise of the Blessed Trinity)

Glory be to the Father, and to the Son, and to the Holy Ghost, as it was in the beginning, is now and ever shall be, world without end. Amen.

The Three Divine Virtues

An Act of Faith.

O my God! I firmly believe all the sacred truths which Thy Holy Catholic Church believes and teaches; because Thou hast revealed them Who canst neither deceive nor be deceived.

An Act of Hope

O my God! relying on Thy infinite goodness and promises, I hope to obtain pardon for my sins, the assistance of Thy grace, and life everlasting, through the merits of Jesus Christ, my Lord and Redeemer.

An Act of Love

O my God! I love Thee above all things with my whole heart and soul because Thou art infinitely amiable, and deserving of all love. I love also my neighbor as myself for the love of Thee. I forgive all who have injured me, and ask pardon of all whom I have injured.

An Act of Contrition

O my God! I am most heartily sorry for all my sins, and I detest them above all things from the bottom of my heart, because they displease Thee, my God, Who art most deserving of all my love for Thy most amiable and adorable perfections. I firmly resolve by Thy holy grace never more to offend Thee, and to do all that I can to atone for my sins, and to amend my life. Amen.

Prayer to the Guardian Angel

O Angel of God! who are my Guardian, to whose care I am committed by the supreme clemency, enlighten, defend, guide, and govern me. Amen.

Morning Devotion

Give your first thought to God, to Jesus in the Blessed Sacrament, and say devoutly: "Jesus, Mary, Joseph, I give you my heart and my soul" (100 days ind.). Remember that thousands of sinners will die on this day, and it may be your last day. Say therefore piously: "My Jesus, have mercy on all the Poor Dying Sinners of this day, and save them from hell. Sweet Heart of Mary, be their salvation. St. Joseph, Patron of a Happy Death, pray for us and the Poor Dying Sinners. Amen." Do not forget the good intention and renew briefly your Act of Consecration by saying with all fervor: "O my God! all for Thy greater honor and glory and the salvation of the Poor Dying Sinners. Amen." If you have time, make the Acts of Adoration, Thanksgiving, Offering, and Petition, as in the following prayer:

Devout Morning Prayer and Offering

O eternal God and ever-blessed Trinity, Father, Son, and Holy Ghost! With all the angels and saints I adore Thy infinite Majesty. Thou art my first beginning and last end. I submit myself to Thy holy will, and I devote myself to Thy divine service now and forever. From the bottom of my heart I thank Thee, most bountiful God, for all the favors and benefits Thou hast bestowed upon me, particularly for having preserved me during the night, and for granting me this day to serve Thee. I earnestly invite all the angels and saints to join with me in praise and thanksgiving for Thy infinite goodness O my God! I offer Thee my whole being all my thoughts, desires, words and actions of this day and of my whole life. I wish to live only for Thee, for Thy greater honor and glory, and the salvation of the Poor Dying Sinners. O good God preserve me today from sin and all evil, and give me the grace, always to fulfill Thy holy will and to please Thee in all my actions. O Jesus! I wish to unite myself with Thee and all the holy Masses that are celebrated today that Thy most precious Blood may continually plead for the Dying Sinners and the Poor Souls in Purgatory. My Jesus, mercy. Amen.

Prayer before Meals
Bless us, O Lord, and these Thy gifts, which we are about to receive from Thy bounty, through Christ, our Lord. Amen. Our Father. . .Hail Mary .

Prayer after Meals
We give The thanks, Almighty God, for these and all Thy benefits, Who livest and reignest world without end. Amen. Our Father ... Hail Mary ...

... And may the souls of the faithful departed through the mercy of God rest in peace. Amen.

Evening Prayers

O my God! Prostrate on my knees, I adore Thee, most Holy Trinity, with all the angels and saints that surround the throne of Thy infinite Majesty. I thank Thee heavenly Father for having created me, I thank Thee, divine Son for having redeemed me, I thank Thee, Holy Ghost for having sanctified me, and called me to Thy Holy Catholic Church. But particularly do I thank Thee for all the graces, favors, and benefits Thou hast bestowed upon me this day. Join me, ye blessed Spirits, in thanking the God of mercies, Who is so bountiful to so unworthy a creature. Come, Holy Ghost, and enlighten my mind that I may clearly see all the sins I have committed this day in thought, word, and action, and give me the grace to obtain full pardon of them by an act of sincere contrition. (After this act of contrition recommend to God all those near and dear to you, but especially the Dying Sinners and the Poor Souls in Purgatory and close with this Prayer of the Church:)
Visit, we beseech Thee, O Lord, this habitation, and drive from it all the snares of the enemy. Let Thy holy Angels dwell therein to preserve us in peace, and may

Thy blessing be upon us forever; through Christ, our Lord. Amen.

Bless, O Lord, the repose I am going to take, in order to renew my strength, that I may be better able to serve Thee. O all ye Saints and Angels, but chiefly thou, O Mother of God, and dear St. Joseph, intercede for me this night and during the rest of my life, but particularly at the hour of my death. May the divine assistance remain always with us. My Jesus, mercy on all those, that will die during this night, and save them from hell. Amen.

Prayer for Mass
(page 95)

N. B. Use the rest of the time between the prayers by saying some decades of the Rosary for the Dying, and meditate a little on the Sacrifice of the Cross, and the Sufferings and Death of Jesus Christ.

Prayer After Mass
(Prescribed by Pope Leo XIII)

Three times the "*Hail Mary*," followed by the *Salve Regina*:

Hail! Holy Queen, Mother of Mercy, our life, our sweetness, and our hope! To thee do we cry, poor banished children of Eve; to thee do we send up our sighs, mourning and weeping in this valley of tears. Turn then most gracious Advocate, thine eyes of mercy toward us, and after this our exile show unto us the blessed fruit of thy womb, Jesus. O clement, O pious, O sweet Virgin Mary!

V. Pray for us, O holy Mother of God.
R. That we may be made worthy of the promises of Christ.

Let us Pray:

God, our refuge and our strength, graciously hear Thy people crying to Thee; and through the intercession of the glorious and Immaculate Virgin Mary, Mother of God, of her spouse, St. Joseph, Thy holy Apostles Peter and Paul, and all the Saints, mercifully and graciously hear our prayers which we offer Thee for the conversion of sinners, and for the liberty and exaltation of Holy Mother Church, through Christ, our Lord. Amen.

Saint Michael, the Archangel, defend us in the conflict. Be our protection against the malice and snares of the devil. Restrain him, O God, we humbly beseech Thee, and do thou, O Prince of the heavenly host, by the divine power cast into hell satan and the other evil spirits that roam through the world, seeking the destruction of souls. Amen.

Most Sacred Heart of Jesus, have mercy on us! (Three times).

Devotions for Confession

In order to prepare well for Confession, we must 1) examine our conscience, that we may know all our sins, at least all mortal sins, committed since our last good Confession. 2) Be truly sorry for having committed them. 3) Firmly resolve never to commit them again. 4) Candidly and humbly confess them to a priest empowered to absolve us. 5) Have the good will of making satisfaction for our sins.

Prayer to the Holy Ghost for a Good Confession
Come, Holy Ghost! enlighten my mind that I may clearly see all my sins by which I have offended the good God. Let not self-love deceive or blind me, but show me the true state of my conscience. Move my heart to sincere contrition for all my sins and help me

to make such a sincere and sorrowful confession of my sins that I may receive a full pardon of them through the merits of Jesus Christ. Amen.

Then examine your conscience carefully and make a good act of contrition (page 140) before you enter the confessional.

Prayer after Confession

I give Thee thanks, O Lord Jesus, that Thou hast been pleased to cleanse me from the stains of my sins. Blessed be Thy name, O Lord, Who dost not reject any one that comes to Thee with a contrite heart, but receivest him into favor and numberest him with Thy children. I adore and praise Thy infinite mercy and devote myself again entirely to Thy service forever. O good God, give me the grace that 1 may avoid sin and all occasions of sin. This I resolve to do by Thy divine help without which I can do nothing. Bless my good resolutions that I may keep them and never offend Thee again. Supply also by Thy mercy whatever defects I have committed in my confession, and help me to make full satisfaction for all my sins. Amen.

After this prayer perform the penance given you by the priest.

Prayers Before and After Holy Communion
(page 94)

Prayer Before a Crucifix to Gain a Plenary Indulgence After Holy Communion

BEHOLD me, O good and amiable Jesus, falling on my knees before Thy face, and with the greatest ardor of my soul praying and beseeching Thee to impress indelibly on my heart lively sentiments of faith, hope and charity, true contrition for my sins and a firm purpose of amendment; while I contemplate with love and tender pity Thy five wounds which recall to my mind the words that David, Thy prophet spoke of

Thee: "They have pierced my hands and my feet, they have numbered all my bones."
(Add a few prayers according to the intention of the Holy Father.)

Do not forget to pray most fervently to Jesus after Holy Communion for the Poor Dying Sinners of that day. "My Jesus, have mercy on the Poor Dying Sinners and save them from hell. Amen."

Divine Praises after Benediction
Blessed be God!
Blessed be His Holy Name!
Blessed be Jesus Christ, true God and true man!
Blessed be the name of Jesus!
Blessed be His Most Sacred Heart!
Blessed be Jesus in the Most Holy Sacrament of the Altar!
Blessed be the great Mother of God, Mary most Holy!
Blessed be her Holy and Immaculate Conception!
Blessed be the name of Mary, Virgin and Mother!
Blessed be St. Joseph, her most chaste Spouse!
Blessed be God, in His Angels and in His Saints!

The Holy Rosary

Let no day pass without saying some part of the Holy Rosary, the prayer most pleasing to Mary. It is composed of fifteen decades, each decade consisting of one Our Father, ten Hail Marys, and one Glory be to the Father, etc. During each decade we should call to mind the mystery of the life of Christ and Mary which the decade is intended to honor.

I. The Five Joyful Mysteries.
1) The Annunciation.
2) The Visitation.
3) The Nativity.
4) The Presentation.
5) The Finding in the Temple.

II. The Five Sorrowful Mysteries.
1) The Agony in the Garden.
2) The Scourging at the Pillar.
3) The Crowning with Thorns.
4) The Carrying of the Cross.
5) The Crucifixion.

III. The Five Glorious Mysteries.
The Resurrection.
The Ascension.

3) The Coming of the Holy Ghost on the Apostles.
4) The Assumption of the Blessed Virgin.
5) The Coronation of the Blessed Virgin.

Devotion to St. Anthony of Padua

St. Anthony of Padua, of the Order of Friars Minor, is called the great Wonder-Worker of our days. A most powerful means to obtain a favor from St. Anthony, is the No vena of nine consecutive Tuesdays. How pleasing will it be to St. Anthony to make the nine Tuesdays for the Poor Dying Sinners to obtain their eternal Salvation and God's blessing on this great work. You may use these prayers:

Prayer to St. Anthony

O glorious St. Anthony, safe refuge of the afflicted and distressed, who by a miraculous revelation has directed all those who seek thy aid to come to thy altar with the promise that whatsoever visits it for nine consecutive Tuesdays and there piously invokes thee, will feel the power of thy intercession; I, a poor sinner, encouraged by this promise come to thee, O powerful Saint, and with a firm hope I implore thy aid, thy protection, thy counsel, and thy blessing. Obtain for me, I beseech thee, my request in this necessity. But if it should be opposed to. the will of God and the welfare of my soul, obtain for me such other graces, as will be conducive to my salvation, through Christ our Lord. Amen.

Prayer to the Infant Jesus in the Arms of St. Anthony.

O Jesus, my Savior! Who didst vouchsafe to appear to St. Anthony in the form of an Infant, I implore Thee, through the love Thou didst bear to this Saint when he dwelt on earth, and which Thou now bears to him in heaven, graciously hear my prayer, and assist me in my necessities, Who livest and reignest, world without end. Amen.

The Responsory of Saint Anthony

V. If miracles thou fain wouldst see:
Lo! error, death, calamity,
The leprous stain, the demon flies, From beds of pain the sick arise.
R. The hungry seas forego their prey, The prisoner's cruel chains give way,
While palsied limbs, and chattels lost,
Both young and old recovered boast.
V. And perils perish; plenty's hoard Is heaped on hunger's famished board.

Let those relate, who know it well, Let Padua of her
Patron tell.
R. The hungry seas forego their etc.
V. May glory to the Father be,
And to the Son eternally,
And to the Spirit, in essence one, In Persons three, be
honor done.
R. The hungry seas forego their etc.
V. Pray for us, Blessed Anthony,
R. That we may be made worthy of the promises of
Christ.

Let us Pray:

O God! Let the votive commemoration of Blessed
Anthony, Thy Confessor, be a source of joy to Thy
Church, that she may always be fortified with spiritual
assistance, and may deserve to possess eternal joy.
Through Christ our Lord. Amen.

Conclusion

Let us be fervent in this devotion for the Dying and
endeavor to propagate it everywhere. Recommend the
souls of your Dying parents, relatives, friends, and
particularly of obstinate sinners to the prayers of the

Confraternity. We shall not repent of it at the hour of our own death. Who knows how soon, perhaps, we ourselves shall need this very same assistance?

THE PIOUS UNION OF ST. JOSEPH

Applications for admission to the Union and the Confraternity may be directed to:

Rev. Director of the Pious Union,
Shrine of St. Joseph
953 East Michigan Avenue
Grass Lake, MI 49240

Public Devotion of the Little Company in a Church

Where the Little Company of St. Joseph meets for a public devotion in the Church, the following order of exercises may be observed:

1. Exposition of the Blessed Sacrament.

2. O SALUTARIS HOSTIA
O Salutaris Hostia!
Quae coeli pandis ostium;
Bella premunt hostilia,
Da robur, fer auxilium.
Uni trinoque Domino
Sit sempiterna gloria,
Qui vitam, sine termino
Nobis donet in patria. Amen.

3. The First and Second Act of Adoration and Petition for the Dying Sinners, as in the Pious Union Book, p. 115 and 116.

4. HYMN TO ST. JOSEPH.
First Verse:
Dear Guardian of Mary!

Dear nurse of her child!
Life's ways are so weary,
 the desert is wild;
Bleak sands all around us,
no home can we see;
Sweet Spouse of our Lady!
we lean upon thee.

5. The Third and Fourth Act of Adoration and Petition for. the Dying Sinners as in the Pious Union Book, p. 117 and 118.

6. HYMN TO ST. JOSEPH.
Second Verse:
For thou to the pilgrim art father and guide,
And Jesus and Mary felt safe at thy side;
Ah! Blessed Saint Joseph, how safe would I be,
Sweet Spouse of our Lady! If thou wert with me.

7. The Fifth Act of Adoration and Petition for the Dying Sinners, Pious Union Book, p. 119.

8. Acts of Consecration of new members at the Communion-Railing, as in the Pious Union Book, p. 6 and 56.

9. Prayers (3 *Paters, Aves, Glorias*) to St. Joseph for the special intentions.
The Litany of St. Joseph, as in the Pious Union Book, p. 53.

10. TANTUM ERGO
Tantum ergo Sacramentum
Veneremur cernui,
Et antiquum documentum Novo cedat ritui;
Praestet fides supplementum Sensuum defectui.
Genitori, Genitoque Laus et Jubilatio,
Salus, honor, virtus quoque
Sit et benedictio,
Procedenti ab utroque
Compar sit laudatio. Amen.

BENEDICTION

11. COME HOLY GHOST.
Come, Holy Ghost, Creator blest,
And in our hearts take up thy rest,
Come with Thy Grace and heavenly aid,
To fill the hearts, which Thou hast made.
To fill the hearts, which Thou hast made.
O Comforter, to Thee we cry;
Thou heavenly Gift of God Most High;
Thou Fount of life and Fire of love,

And sweet anointing from above.
And sweet anointing from above.
12. An address by the Director either in the Church or at
the Meeting in the Hall.

CPSIA information can be obtained
at www.ICGtesting.com
Printed in the USA
LVHW050607160723
752317LV00005B/6/J